THE SH!T NO ONE TELLS YOU ABOUT TODDLERS

The

SH!T

NO ONE TELLS YOU ABOUT

TODDLERS

A Guide to Surviving the Toddler Years
DAWN DAIS

SEAL PRESS

Copyright 2015 Dawn Dais

Seal Press
A Member of the Perseus Books Group
1700 Fourth Street
Berkeley, California
sealpress.com

Library of Congress Cataloging-in-Publication Data is available.

ISBN: 978-1-58005-589-5

10 9 8 7 6 5 4 3 2 1

Cover design by Kimberly Glyder
Interior design by Megan Jones Design
Illustrations by Dawn Dais
Photo Vivian and Daniel on page v © Dan Hood Photography

Printed in the United States of America
Distributed by Publishers Group West

To Vivian and Daniel, for always providing content

Contents

$\mathcal{W}$ ELCOME (BACK), DEAR readers! When we last spoke you were up to your eyeballs in the joys of new parenthood (joy smells a lot like spit-up and pureed peas, it turns out). In my last book, *The Sh!t No One Tells You: A Guide to Surviving Your Baby's First Year,* I helped new parents through the first year with their babies. In that book I implied that kids got easier after their first year. Dear readers, that was a lie.

In my defense, when I wrote that book I was in possession of only one eighteen-month-old child, who had not yet fully embraced her Wrath of the Toddler. I had no idea what wonders still awaited me on this parenting adventure. I apologize that I didn't warn you sooner.

The Wrath of the Toddler is most commonly associated with the Terrible Twos but, and this is fantastic news, the actual terrible time can extend well before and after that one magical year. I'm sorry to be the one to break this to you.

The word "toddler" is derived from how the child looks when he or she first enters this time—toddling away. It all starts so adorably, doesn't it? Most parents are excited when their kid starts toddling, because walking seems to mark an end of babyhood and the beginning of the exciting "kid" years. And those parents are right: it is exciting to see your little blob of baby slowly start to become a real live person.

But just as you are celebrating your survival of Baby Days by purging all things breastfeeding and binky, your sweet child is quietly becoming possessed by the devil. Or, as some like to call it, "becoming a real live person." You forgot that most real live people are a-holes, didn't you? You really should have taken that into greater consideration before you went and acquired one of your own.

While this baby of yours spent those first months clinging to you with every tiny fiber of might, the toddler years are the beginning of the decades-long journey to independence. This can be hard on both children and parents because it marks such a change in your overall dynamic. I remember in the case of my son that he seemed to literally become a different kid right around the time he started walking. Which meant I all of a sudden had to recalibrate how to be his parent.

Like many a toddler who toddled before him, my Daniel was delighted to discover the joys of standing upright and couldn't wait to see how far this new skill could take him. Unfortunately for his poor bruised head, he had to learn the hard way that his body wasn't quite able to keep up with his ambition.

This is where I have found most of the Wrath of the Toddler occurs, in the frustration tots feel from not being able to expedite that independence as fast as their little brains want to. There's frustration in store for the parent as well, because one minute you're marveling at how big your little baby is getting and the next minute you're wondering how it is scientifically possible for one (tiny) human being to access such a range of emotions in the span of thirty-five seconds. Holy mood swings, Batman.

I've found a few things to be really helpful in trying to wrap my mind around the toddler years. The first and most important thing I constantly remind myself is that, although my toddlers are getting bigger, they are still essentially just monkeys in cute clothes (which also explains why they always want to take their clothes off). Until said children can speak rationally to me, wipe their own butts, and sit through an entire meal without feeling overcome with the urge to throw their plates, I do not consider them actual human children.

It may sound mean to compare children to monkeys (because monkeys seem really sweet), but I promise you this mindset will help bring everything into focus. It will help explain the child's lack of communication skills (pointing and screaming is textbook monkey) and baffling behavior (feral primates would also be endlessly entertained by sporting Tupperware on their heads). Most important, this truth keeps your reflexes sharp, as everyone knows it can get ugly when monkeys start throwing things.

If you ever get confused about where your child falls on the journey to becoming an Actual Human Child, I've outlined the progression below:

Blob ➤ *Smiling Blob* ➤ *Monkey* ➤ *Angry Monkey* ➤ *Actual Human Child*

It's just science, really.

Once you've accepted that you're living with a monkey you can also implement my second helpful tip. This tip is to always treat your monkey as though it is armed and very dangerous. Make no sudden movements. Proceed with caution. And for the love of God, don't go cutting any food in any manner unless you've confirmed with the monkey at least seven times that the cut is indeed desired. Even then, always be on high alert following any and all food alteration.

My third tip for surviving the toddler years is to look for those handy carrying cases at the store that offer you a discount if you buy six bottles of wine at once. That's part of the science as well.

My fourth tip is to find other moms who are dealing with their own moody monkeys. They will offer you support, humor, ideas, and most likely, some of their wine. Mom friends are the best.

To help you along with my fourth tip I've once again enlisted the help of some of my mom friends to share their advice and stories about surviving the toddler years. They are my Moms on the Front Lines, and you'll be hearing from them throughout the book. They are the soldiers out there fighting the good fight as we all try to somehow turn these little monkeys into respectable members of society. And by "respectable members" we mean "members who don't regularly throw themselves onto the floor in public." We like to keep our missions attainable, you see.

So come along as we head off on a whole new stage of parenting. There will be laughter and tears, heartache, and well-fought victories. And that's just dinnertime.

The toddler years have arrived, and I'm going to give you all the humor, heart, and honesty you need to survive them. Yay, moms!

(Sorry, wine sold separately.)

MY MOMS ON THE FRONT LINES

*T*HEY SAY PARENTING is the hardest job you'll ever love. But I like to think of it more as the hardest job you can't ever quit. So it's actually more like a life sentence than a career, if you think about it. But you probably shouldn't think about it.

Since we're all in for the long haul I find great comfort and comradery in my friends who are moms. I love picking their brains about their experiences, their highs and lows, their successes and wonderfully disastrous failures. They give me ideas and support, but mostly they give me relief. It's so incredibly helpful to hear other moms tell me how hard this all is. Because so often I start to think I'm the only parent on the planet who is overwhelmed.

As I did in my first *Sh!t* book, I've once again included my ragtag bunch of Moms on the Front Lines, or MOFL, as I refer to them. I think they help bring home the whole point of this book: you are not alone. My moms have come to share with you their insights, advice, and experiences, but mostly they're here to say, "Me too." Sometimes a little "Me too" is all we need to get through a particularly harrowing day of herding toddlers. Misery, meet your company.

What I love most about my group of moms is how different we all are, and yet, in the end, the same. Some of us are married, some single, some going through divorce. Some of us work full-time, some of us stay at home with the kids. We're all in our thirties and forties, but we all feel like we're in our eighties. We're all good moms with a good sense of humor about how ridiculously hard it is to be a good mom. And we're all doing our best on an unacceptably low amount of sleep.

A lot of different moms contribute throughout the book. Here's a brief rundown of the names you'll see pop up most often:

ME, DAWN: We have two kids, Daniel, eighteen months, and Vivian, almost four years old. We are done having kids because we're not strong enough to endure the consequences of being outnumbered by the little people in our house. I've seen enough sci-fi movies to know what happens when the machines take over. My partner, Becky, and I have been together eight years. We both work from home part- to full-time depending on our workloads. We have two cats, two dogs, and a horse that Becky rescued because we have nothing else going on in our lives.

BROOKE: We've been married five years and have two kids. A girl three and a half years old and a boy, two years old. I previously worked full-time. Then part-time after the first baby, and now I am at home full-time. I am married and my husband works from home two to three days a week and travels overnight at least once a week. We are done with kids!!

DANA: We've been married for ten years. We have one girl (four years old) and one boy (two years old). I'm 90 percent sure our family is complete. Both my husband and I work full-time (or more). We are lucky to have family that live close by to help with our demanding schedules, in addition to our daycare provider, whom I consider my children's second mom and part of the family. She loves them like her own and is vital to our ability to function as a family the way we do!

DEANNA: Married ten years in July. We have three kids: seven, four, and two. We both work full-time. We are done having kids. I work where my kids go to school. Since I have to work, it has been a huge blessing to be able to have them close to me throughout the day.

(STILL) CHIPPER JEN: Recently divorcing, single mom. Two beautiful, resilient children, ages six and four, who don't deserve a broken home but are taking it like champs! I left my career to stay home and raise babies because that's what I believe is my calling. Now I'm looking to juggle a full-time job, school, and mom/dad duties due to my ex's horrible choices. Hoping to get through it all in one piece with therapy and wine!

JILL: I'm married with nine-year-old boy/girl twins. I stayed at home until kids started first grade and then went back to teaching full-time. Considering we had a rough pregnancy and delivered at twenty-seven weeks, no more kids.

KAREN: I'm a single mom of a five-and-a-half-year-old girl, and I'm working full-time! I'm pretty sure I'm done with having kids unless my love life miraculously changes in the next year or so. Balancing a fifty-plus-hour workweek and taking care of my daughter full-time are only possible because I have the help and support of my amazing family, who live close by.

KAYSEE: I've been married eight years. We have three kids: one boy, age seven, and two girls, ages five and a half and two. Our plan is to be done. We are business owners with a very flexible work schedule. My husband works full-time and I work part-time.

MICHAELA: I've been married for four years. One two-year-old boy, and a girl on the way. Two kids and done . . . plus the wild, lunatic dog we love, but who is as much work as the toddler. We both work full-time.

MICHELLE: I have two boys, ages four and two. I recently became a stay-at-home mom (due to the place where I worked going out of business) and am loving every minute of it, although I am looking for part-time work that is flexible. I have been married for eight years to a very hard working (fifty to sixty hours a week) engineer. We are done having kids.

SARAH B.: Two boys (five and a half and two and a half), one dog (eight), two cats (sixteen and fourteen), and one tortoise (fiftyish)! We have been married eight and a half years, but have been together twenty years this past November. We both work full-time. I work four ten-hour days, so I have three days with the boys. We are done, due to surgical procedures. But I would have loved to have one more.

SARAH G.: We've been married fourteen and a half years; we both work full-time. We employ a village to help care for our kids and keep the household running. We have four kids, ages eleven, eight and a half, four and a half, and eighteen months. DONE. For real this time. There will be no postscript! *(Note from Dawn: In my last book, Sarah proclaimed they were done having kids after three, then she had an oopsie and now she has four.)* Oh: we also have one dog that we love but is a pain in my arse. And a cat that I don't love but she's a great mouser.

TARA: We've been married seven years and have a two-year-old boy as well as a golden retriever (also male). I work part-time as a special education teacher. We plan to have one more child, unless that one more child is another boy. In that case we will either try for a girl or I will buy myself a sweet puppy named Ella.

THE PROFESSIONAL MOMS

In addition to my Moms on the Front Lines, this time around I've included the opinions of two professionals throughout the book. Moms in the Therapist Office, as it were. Personally, I like to mix professional opinions with the opinions of my friends and family (and of course the Internet) when I'm tackling parenting issues. Given that there are so many different ways to go about things, I always hope that the more opinions I gather, the greater chance I have of finding one that actually works.

Also, so much of toddler behavior can be explained by what's going on developmentally in their ever-expanding brains. Our two professionals are able to offer some insight into toddler development that might be slightly more based in research than my Monkey Theory. If you can imagine that.

Both of these women were so helpful and open in addressing the various topics I threw their way. I know you will love what they have to say throughout the book. Read a little more about their experience below and check out their websites for more information on how to connect with them.

KATIE HURLEY, LCSW, is a child and adolescent psychotherapist and writer in Los Angeles, California. Her work can be found on *The Huffington Post* and on several popular online parenting sites, including www.Momtastic.com, www.mom.me, www.EverydayFamily.com, and her own Practical Parenting (www.practicalkatie.com). She is the author of the parenting book *The Happy Kid Handbook: How to Raise Joyful Children in a Stressful World* (Tarcher/Penguin). Katie enjoys life by the beach with her husband and two children.

GAIL MARIE POVERMAN-KAVE, LCSW, has been in private practice since 1990. She specializes in working with children and adolescents and their families. She also provides educational presentations to volunteer, civic, school, and corporate groups on topics such as effective communication, self-esteem, and the positive power of humor. Gail is the mom of thirteen-year-old boy/girl twins. Her website is www.gailpovermankave.com.

THE SH!T NO ONE TELLS YOU ABOUT TODDLERS

1

YOU SUCK AT THIS

It's not just your imagination

GETTING OUT THE DOOR

CHILD(REN) MORNING CHECKLIST
(only two allowed, on a good day)

☐ Get out of bed
  (without tears)

☐ Get dressed
  (without kicking mommy in the face)

☐ Eat breakfast
  (while sitting at the table)

☐ Brush teeth
  (without being chased)

☐ Put on shoes
  (both shoes)

☐ Get in the car
  (without having to be bribed)

I'M A BIG fan of routine. Of solving problems. Of order and logic. Unfortunately, I am also a parent. In my non-parent life, I've done pretty well for myself by putting my mind to certain skills or tasks, learning how to do them, figuring out strategies for success. These strategies tend to work over and over again, after initial periods of trial and error. Sadly, the same techniques that bring me success for everything else in my life are absolute crap when applied to parenting. Most of the time all I feel like I'm doing is error-ing.

I don't like sucking at things, and most of the time I overwhelmingly feel like I suck at any and all attempts to parent effectively. I feel like those poor scientists who develop the flu vaccine every year only to have the flu virus mutate into something they didn't protect against. Just when I get a handle on the particular phase my kids are going through, they get bored and move on to some other way of making me feel incompetent.

When I had my second kid, I figured everything I learned from Attempt #1 would surely apply to Attempt #2. I was so disappointed to discover that kids are actually individuals with different personalities, and therefore I couldn't just reuse most of my previous knowledge. This was the most disheartening of discoveries.

I remember distinctly a time when we were having a rough patch with Vivian. Putting her down at night was getting to be an hours-long undertaking. (Please see Chapter 8: You May Be Too Tired to Sleep Train This Child.) My partner and I were absolutely exhausted from nights spent trying to wrangle the child into bed before 11:00 PM. On this particular night Vivian had been screaming in her crib for quite some time, so we brought her into our bed to try to reset her with a little hypnotic BabyFirst Nighttime TV. This strategy stopped her crying, yes, but now Vivian was running around the house with delight while we lay facedown on our bed, so *so* ready to sleep. It was 11:30 PM. I screamed into my comforter, "Why do we suck so bad at this???!!!"

Keep in mind that Vivian was not a newborn—we had been at this parenting thing for going on two years. It was completely unacceptable that we had not figured out what the hell was going on. The kid was not all right. Or at the very least the moms weren't.

As Vivian has gotten older, and now that I've started all over with Attempt #2, I've come to realize how quickly kids move through different phases. With my first kid everything felt endless, even if it only lasted days. If we were having a particularly bad stretch, I would get overwhelmed by thinking that it was somehow going to last forever—that somehow Vivian would refuse to go to bed before midnight for the rest of her life. It sounds ridiculous when I type it, but it always felt very real at the time. Sucking at something and having absolutely no idea how to get better at it is a tremendously overwhelming feeling for a control freak like me.

So instead of trying to master particular parenting challenges I started focusing on mastering my reaction to the challenges. I try not to let myself get too upset when we hit a rough patch, not to let myself drown in that overwhelming feeling I get when things aren't going well. I know now that it will pass; sometimes it'll even pass in a few minutes if I don't let it get me too worked up.

When Daniel is having a long stretch of horrible teething nights, I constantly remind myself that his sister is sleeping peacefully in the next room: the same sister who required one of us in her room for hours at a time throughout her teething battles. Yes, sometimes it will be days or weeks or even years before we come out of the woods, but somehow knowing that eventually we will be out helps me stay calm. There is also a small possibility that the past four years of not sleeping has just made me too exhausted to get worked up anymore.

Maybe I'll patent my new Exhaustion Zen method and teach my technique to the masses. I'll share it with you here.

STEP 1: Stop sleeping.

STEP 2: Add children.

STEP 3: Stare blankly at an unmoving focal point when life starts to stress you out.

Voilà! Inner peace!

Oprah, call me. This is revolutionary.

Moms on the Front Lines

WE ARE HORRIBLE PARENTS

Seeking reassurance that I am not the only one who sucks at parenting, I reached out to my MOFL. They did not disappoint.

Deanna, mom of three, made me feel better, because she's been failing even longer than I have. She said: "The other night I looked at my husband and said, 'We've been doing this for seven years! How are we so bad at this?!'"

Michelle also felt my pain. "Just when I relax and think, 'I can do this!' one of my kids goes and hurts himself. The kids are ever changing, which is exciting and frustrating at the same time. I just try to remember that whatever awful stage they're in won't last forever and try to focus on the positive. Also, a glass of wine always helps!"

Michaela shared a common parent failing. "I think we always feel a little bit like we're 'sucking at this,' but I've come to realize that's part of being a first-time parent. We once drove all the way to Vallejo and discovered Sam was not buckled into his car seat. Man, I suck at this."

I've had a car seat mishap too. I buckled the kid in the seat but, because the seat had been used in another car recently, I didn't realize it wasn't actually buckled *to* the car. Details are hard. I swerved to miss another car, and there slid the seat and the child across the backseat. Oopsie.

Sarah B. felt like she sucks on a daily basis. "It's a rare occasion when I actually feel like I am doing an okay job. More often than not I find myself surrounded by a screaming, crying,

➤

barking chaos. Oh, and I have also driven without Drew buckled into his seat. I was sobbing when I told my husband about it that night. Such great memories."

Deanna detailed her morning attempts at order. "I suck at parenting, especially in the mornings when I'm trying to get everyone up, ready, and out the door on time. Usually my goal is to accomplish this simple daily task without screaming or having anyone in tears. I have come to *hate* mornings because I suck at them. There have been a few miraculous mornings when I was able to get the three kids and myself dressed, fed, teeth and hair brushed, and belongings in hand with no one screaming or crying. I think I was successful twice this year . . . yay, me!"

Stories like these make my heart happy. Not because we are all horrible parents, and should quite possibly be incarcerated for our poor car seat skills, but because they make me feel so much less alone in my own suckage. When both of the kids are melting down, food is flying, baths are being fought, or we have run out of our go-to bribery fruit snacks, Becky always looks at me and says, "Are we the only ones who are this bad at parenting?"

Knowing that other parents—people I *know* are good parents—are also struggling means that I can exclaim, "No!! We *all* suck!!" This makes me feel better, even if it means all our children are doomed.

(Ignore this section, Oprah.)

2

WALKING IS HARD

Bruising is considerably less difficult

TODDLER ATTIRE

"Sorry, bud, but if you get one more head injury someone is surely going to take me to prison. I'll see if I can find Thomas the Train bubble wrap for you."

$\mathcal{W}$HEN MOST OF us think of toddlers, of course, we usually think of their attitudes and temper tantrums. And yet, the word "toddle" perfectly describes how they look when they first enter this exciting time in their lives. At least it perfectly described my bounding baby boy who started "walking" on his first birthday. Why am I putting *walking* in quotes? Would I be considered "flying" if I only "flew" for three seconds before I plummeted to the ground? Probably not. Daniel was a short-distance walker at best. But what he lacked in coordination he made up for in really bad reflexes.

Poor Daniel did not have an easy time of it when he first started his toddling. *Bam!* The fact that we had hardwood floors did not help his situation. *Bam!* Daniel's forehead met the floor every five minutes. *Bam!* I'm not exaggerating to say the child had a bruise on his head (in various states and sizes) for six solid months. The boy looked so incredibly battered I started pointing out the bruises to strangers when we were out in public. My thinking was, if I were actually abusing him I wouldn't talk so freely about his injuries.

I asked Daniel's doctor at what point I should officially become alarmed that he was falling on his head 358 times a day. The doctor answered, "As long as he's not going unconscious he should be fine."

I looked at her in shock. Really?! That's my line in the sand?!

Chipper Jen had a similar experience at the doctor's office. "I remember the doctor saying something about, before the age of two, the plates in kids' heads actually kinda shift if they hit their heads. I was concerned about Austin literally having brain damage from falling on his head *all* the time. But he's fine!!!"

- -

This was all such new territory for me. Of course Vivian had had her share of tumbles when she first started walking, but they were nothing compared to Daniel's. The boy seemed to have absolutely no regard for his health and safety. Where Vivian was cautious and deliberate, Daniel just barreled ahead without a second thought as to how his attempts at coordination were going to feel when they failed. Things were meant to be climbed on, his legs were meant for running, and gravity was his enemy. It didn't help matters that his head size was in the ninety-eighth percentile. He was like a Q-tip running around trying to hold his big ol' head up. Again, gravity working against him.

We had moved into a two-story house shortly before Vivian started walking. We never had to put up a gate at either end of the stairs to keep her safe. We taught her how to climb up and down the stairs, and she was always fine. She would slowly navigate those stairs and took each step with all her concentration. Other parents would come over to our house and look at our stairs in absolute horror as if they were a death trap. We silently judged their out-of-control children.

Then came Daniel.

Now we have four gates in our house, all an attempt to corral this crazy boy. Vivian just shakes her head at how out of control he is. It's so funny to me that I have such a stereotypical girl and a stereotypical boy. I've never thought much of gender stereotypes, probably because I was such a tomboy growing up and couldn't (and still can't) be bothered with most "girl" things. But here are these two kids, being raised the exact same way, with completely different motors.

I asked my professionals if it's true that boys and girls are different. They both poo-pooed the idea, stating that personality was a more deciding factor than gender.

Katie Hurley says, "Some kids seem to enter this world with big personalities and a need to push their own physical boundaries, while others hang back and enjoy the ride. Try not to get caught up in the gender of it all. It's more about getting to know what makes your child tick than whether your child is a girl or a boy."

Gail Marie Poverman-Kave also thinks I'm off-base in my thinking that Daniel's gender has anything to do with the fact that he is insane. "There are many beliefs in our country about boys being wild, impulsive risk takers and girls being calm, patient care givers. There is mounting evidence to suggest that much of what we see and believe in this country is largely a result of parenting and cultural expectations."

Gail thinks that some of our children's behavior can be linked to how we parent them. That parents instinctually act differently toward boys than they do toward girls. Personally, Gail is raising her two children to be people first, and their gender second. "Perhaps this approach," she told me, "could greatly diminish some of the wild behaviors that we tend to see in boys."

I would really like to side with science on this one, but I don't think the differences in my children have anything to do with how they are being raised. Vivian is being raised by two mommies. One of her mommies can throw a ball farther than some boys. She had stereotypical "boy" toys since birth and has been made to watch sports and go fishing with Grandpa. And yet, she is still my gentle little girl who will *always* pick a dress over any other clothes. And Daniel loves dolls and shoes, but he will *always* choose to risk his life climbing on things rather than sit still for longer than thirty seconds at a time.

I asked my MOFL if they felt like their boys were crazier than their girls. Or how the two genders varied, if at all, in their households.

Brooke, mom of one boy and one girl, feels my pain. "Ugh! Where to begin?"

Leah has two boys who run circles around their sister. "The girls will be coloring quietly for half an hour while the boys destroy the whole house."

Sarah G., with one girl and three boys, doesn't see as many stereotypical "girl" characteristics in her daughter. "Bea is being raised around a lot of boys—in our home but also all the boys in the court. So, she isn't as stereotypically 'girlie.' She loves princesses and sparkles, etc., but she's also all about zombies and being wild! I think some stuff is gender, but I also think kids just have different dispositions."

I definitely agree that disposition plays a much bigger role in a kid's overall character than gender. I'm happy that both of my kids will grow up in a house that lets them be whomever they want, and provides them each with the same toys and opportunities.

I'm just gonna buy a couple of extra helmets for the boy . . .

Journal Entry

WELCOME HOME!

Becky has been out of town for a few days. She flew up to Washington State to hang out with one of our friends, then the two of them planned a relaxing road trip through Oregon and California to get back to our home. It's rare that one of us is gone, and it can be difficult juggling two kids with only one parent home.

But Becky is coming home today and I feel like I've really kicked the crap out of this parenting thing while she was gone. We had no major meltdowns (me or the children), we accomplished daily goals like getting dressed and bathing without incident, and we even ventured out into the actual world without Mommy rethinking her entire existence. Brava!

Becky has texted to let me know that she is almost home. Our friend she is traveling with will be staying in our spare bedroom. That bedroom doubles as our downstairs diaper-changing station, so I decide to empty out the diaper pail before our guest arrives. You know, to class the place up a bit.

When I open up the back door to take the diaper bag out, the kids dart outside to play. This is fine, as the backyard was designed for them to play freely. And it will only be a minute or so before I call them back in. As I walk back from the trash can I see Daniel playing on the tiny little toddler slide thing in the middle of the lawn. Vivian wants to play too, but needs her shoes. I tell her I'll grab them for her.

As I walk back inside I pass a lawn chair that is normally not left out unattended while the kids are playing. I had left it out today after I sat in it to watch Vivian in her sand box. I don't think anything of the chair. I'll probably sit in it again after I grab Vivi her shoes.

I walk into the house and to the coat closet by the front door. This walk literally takes about three seconds. I hear a *THUD*, then I hear a Daniel Is Really Really Hurt Shriek. Daniel does a lot of shrieking these days, so I've come to recognize what each shriek stands for. His shriek repertoire includes Frustrated, Sad, Angry, Hungry, Confused, and Really Really Hurt. The Really Really Hurt Shriek is loud, then really really quiet as he catches his breath for breaking the sound barrier with his I'm Not Kidding Shriek.

When I'd left Daniel he was on the little slide. Even if he had fallen off that, it was really short and the grass wouldn't have made him scream like this. I sprint back through the house and find him lying on the cement, with the lawn chair tipped over next to him. Vivian is standing near him, her eyes as wide as saucers. In the literally three seconds I've been gone he ran over to the chair, climbed up on it, stood up on it, then flipped it back down to the cement. Oh, dear Lord.

I pick him up in a panic. He is panicking as well. There is blood everywhere. It is coming out of his nose and his mouth. I take him inside and put him on the counter while I wash off his face. All he wants is for me to hold him.

Becky texts, WE JUST PULLED UP.

I text back, COME INSIDE NOW. BLOOD EVERYWHERE.

Becky comes into the house after her relaxing vacation to find Daniel's face and my white T-shirt covered in blood. She freaks the hell out.

"We need to take him to the emergency room, let's go, we have to go now." She is spinning like a top. I am trying to calm her down. Daniel and Vivian are both crying, Daniel shrieking at the sight of his own blood.

Daniel has spent the previous few months doing nothing but falling on his head. He would usually cry after he fell; sometimes he would even do a Daniel-Is-Hurt Shriek. But each time he would be recovered after about ten seconds, ready to take off on his next tumbling adventure.

But not this time. This time he Will. Not. Stop. Shrieking. It is soul-crushing and heartbreaking.

I calm Becky down enough to convince her that a call to the advice nurse might yield quicker results than sitting in an emergency room with a kid who only has a bloody nose.

After a twenty-minute call with the advice nurse listing various things to check on the child, it is determined that Daniel has a bloody nose. And perhaps should be kept away from high things that can tip over near cement.

I collapse on the couch, holding my bloody boy against my shirt, which looks like I lost a knife fight. We all take deep breaths and try to regain our composure. I look over and see my friend, who has just driven on that peaceful road trip with Becky, sitting on the couch, looking a little white.

I laugh and say, "Welcome to our humble home!"

3

YOUR JUDGING OF OTHER PARENTS COMES BACK TO HAUNT YOU

Prepare to eat your words, with a side of karma's a bitch

BREAKDOWN ON AISLE 3

$\mathcal{B}$EFORE YOU HAVE kids, when you see a child having a tantrum in a public place, you likely silently judge the parent, thinking: "Get it together, lady. Your kid is a disaster."

After you have kids, if you see a mom dealing with a "disaster" in the grocery store, your instinct will likely be to head to the liquor aisle to buy her a bottle of wine. And a straw.

If you have a toddler, it is inevitable that someday you will be that mother in the store (or the park, or preschool drop-off, or a dressing room, or your own friggin' driveway) whose child has forgotten how to be a functioning human being. When tantrums start to happen, especially the first couple of times, they will be nearly incomprehensible. "What? Why? You were so happy just a minute ago. Where did we go wrong? Are the fluorescent lights scrambling your brain?"

You start to think, "Is this my karma for judging other parents for so many years? Do I have to repent by suffering through as many breakdowns as I rolled my eyes at?" The answer is yes.

When your kid first enters the Tantrum Years, and demonstrates such in public, you will be horrified, confused, and panic-stricken. First you will try to rationalize with the child. When that fails you will look around in horror, wanting to hide (yourself or the child) in a discount bin to avoid anyone seeing you failing so completely at parenting. Your heart will be racing, your face will be bright red, and your hands will be shaking. No, this isn't a heart attack. It is the next three to fifteen years of your life.

There are decisions to be made once a public tantrum starts. These decisions have a lot to do with (1) how many times you've previously dealt with your child losing his or her mind in public, and (2) how close you are to being done with the intended task.

If you have limited experience dealing with your child's tantrums, your first instinct may be to flee the scene (with or without the child) as soon as things start to go sideways. Over time, as your tolerance for insanity grows, your priorities may shift as well, producing such announcements as: "Sorry everyone, I know he's a pain, but we're out of toilet paper and milk, so I'm not abandoning ship."

The good news is, once you've survived the first few tantrums you'll start to build up an immunity. Yes, dear reader: your child is essentially a flu bug you will have to build up a resistance to. In my case, my little boy started having random screaming fits around his first birthday. He was so happy-go-lucky before that. I actually took him to the doctor, because I was worried something was wrong. Maybe he had an ear infection or some other such ailment causing him pain, which in turn made him cause me pain. The doctor said he was fine and diagnosed him with being a one-year-old. So helpful.

Now, six months later, when the boy starts screaming as I'm pushing him through the grocery store, I just say, "Ah, I know, life is hard." And I keep pushing. And he keeps screaming. It's a special time together that I will cherish always.

This approach is a little more Zen than I was at the beginning. When my sweet Vivian entered her Tantrum Years, I was still under the impression that I was in control of every situation, and I wasn't going to give up that control without a fight. Spoiler alert: there were quite a few fights. She would start to rebel, I would push back and demand she mind me, she would dig in her heels, and things would take off from there. It seems so ridiculous as I type it now—how completely flustered I would get over the actions of a person two and a half feet tall who had the mental capacity of a well-educated Pomeranian (who wasn't housebroken). But oh my goodness did I get upset. I mean, imagine if your Pomeranian just up and started yelling, "No!" at you one day while nipping at your hand. This was an entirely different dynamic from what my chill little baby had gotten me used to.

During more than one dressing attempt gone wrong I was known to grab the child, hold her down, and force clothes on her, while saying, "I am bigger than you, and I will be bigger than you for quite a while, so you should probably stop fighting me." This strategy is highly recommended by all the professionals, I'm sure of it. It was a super successful strategy too; it definitely didn't make the child act even more insane, or result in any fat lips from her flailing her limbs near my face. My well-educated Pomeranian packed a punch.

Over time I came to realize that I had given birth to children who are as stubborn as I am. Which actually helped me in dealing with them. Getting engaged in a battle of the wills is never going to have a peaceful ending. And the second I get angry, I am officially engaged. These days my primary goal is to stay calm—or at the very least give the impression of calm—when the children start losing their minds. A lot of times the fact that I'm not going along on their crazy train is enough to derail it, or at the very least slow it down. So much of what toddlers (or any humans, for that matter) do is because of the reaction it will get from adults. If their mental breakdown is being ignored by Mommy, it starts to lose its appeal. That's not to say that it doesn't sometimes take them a while to realize they don't have an audience. "Is she *still* screaming in there? She has focus, I'll give her that."

Another tool I've used in dealing with tantrums is trying to avoid them in the first place. As I get to know my kids I get to know their triggers, the things that are most likely to send them careening off into a psychotic break. I've gotten better at seeing those things coming and trying to maneuver away from them in time.

If Vivian asks me for something concerning her food, especially if her request involves altering or cutting the food in any way, I always ask her to confirm her decision at least five times before I go ahead with the request. I've been given the "what is cut can't be uncut" lesson too many times. When I see Daniel starting to get frustrated because he's unable to do something, I remind him that he can ask for help instead of screaming at a pitch unlike anything I've ever heard from something other than large machinery. Giving him an alternative to screaming resets his brain, calms him down, and results in the cutest "Helwp pweese" I have ever heard in all my days.

I also try to be prepared when going to places that require children to be respectable human beings. That means I don't go around naptime, because that's a horrible combo platter that will lead to a huge crap sandwich. I bring snacks and toys to help distract them. If we are in the grocery store, I will go to the produce section first and stock up on fruit that they can snack on while we shop. As soon as my daughter was old enough to play games on my phone I would gladly hand it over to entertain her. I know allowing kids to play with handheld devices can be bad for their brains, but I say: if electronics help keep everyone sane, then it's worth the risk. Because Mommy leaving them in the store can't be good for their mental well-being either. Just ask Punky Brewster.

Overall, my biggest success in curbing tantrums has been to try to avoid direct confrontation with my kids when at all possible. When I break it down I can see that the majority of my kids' tantrums or meltdowns are the result of two things: (1) feeling like they aren't in control, and (2) feeling exhausted and not having the emotional reserves to deal with even the slightest hiccup. I can actually relate to both.

So I give them options, so they feel like they have a little control. I also try not to raise my voice when we're heading toward possible disagreement, because the second they sense I'm trying to force them to do something they immediately dig in their heels, trying not to lose control. I've also gotten in the habit of padding all departure times by about twenty minutes. Toddlers instinctively know when you need them to move quickly, and nothing will bring your little ball of energy to a screeching, couldn't-possibly-move halt more than an approaching departure time. "I'm not a Vivi, I'm a kitty, meow."

When none of my tricks works and it's inevitable there'll be a battle of the wills, I usually start with: "Please be a good girl, I really don't want to get upset with you, I know you can do this." Or maybe I'll start counting. (Why does this work? Are children born with a natural fear of sequential numbers?) Finally, if all else fails, I will land on the tried and true: "Do you want to do this the easy way, or the hard way?" Because apparently I get some of my best parenting techniques from the Sopranos.

I will say that the only way the easy/hard threat works is if you've completely lost your cool at some point previously—something I highly recommend doing when you get the chance. And while I'm not talking about getting *crazy* crazy (let's keep

Child Protective Services out of this), it is always good to keep your kids on their toes, and a little loud screaming fit from Mommy tends to do the trick. (Why should toddlers be the only ones who get to scream?) I'm all for being calm and parenting with empathy and logic, but I also believe that sometimes my kids need to just do what I say because I'm the mom and I'm telling them to. And guess what? I'm bigger than them and will be for quite a while.

Bring on the crazed Pomeranians.

Moms on the Front Lines

PUBLIC TODDLER MELTDOWNS

Asking my MOFL for some toddler horror stories made them a bit overwhelmed. I think they had trouble figuring out which story to pick, as they all start to blur together over time.

Deborah, mom of *five* (!!), couldn't even begin to single out one moment of children gone wrong. She has "years and years' worth."

Colleen recounted navigating a store with her crazy child. "Meltdown in the grocery store because he couldn't eat the yogurt in the shopping cart, followed by screaming at the butcher shop because he decided that the fan was evil and trying to kill him (note: last week he was in love with the exact same fan), then screaming on the drive home because he wanted the take-and-bake pizza NOW (also note: he couldn't see the pizza, but knew it was in the car). This was all washed away as soon as we got home. As soon as I opened his door he was all giggles and cuteness. I think my two-year-old is bipolar."

Jill had an adventure in a fast food "jungle gym." "I took the twins to a McDonald's with a giant indoor play structure. Noah freaked out when he got to the top, so I had to worm my way, crawl, and squeeze up to the very top, and then coax him while working us back down to the bottom. My clothes were disheveled, my hair a mess, and every person in the place was looking at me. Minutes later, he crawled back up, giggling. Sigh."

Michelle can't narrow it down. "There wasn't a specific incident, but my oldest was impossible to take shopping from the age of nine months to around two years old. He refused to sit in a shopping cart and always wanted to run. My shopping trips had to be five minutes or less, so there was no browsing. I had to make short, detailed lists and run through the store."

Dana, mom of two, made the mistake of venturing out with both children to a nice store. "I took them to the Nordstrom kids' shoe department. Somehow the kids both peacefully got new shoes and a balloon, then the rest of the trip was absolutely miserable. They both ran circles around people (Rory was barefoot), squealed at a very high pitch, crawled around on the floor, accidently hit people with the balloons they got from the fun shoe department, and basically shut off their ears from being able to hear my voice at all. I was outnumbered, and they knew it! I was too scared to make eye contact with anyone around me. Unfortunately, I think I will be doing my shopping solely online until they're in college." Now that I think about it, Amazon.com might owe a good part of their fortune to the fact that toddlers are a pain in the ass to take out in public. Their slogan should be: "Why risk it? We deliver right to your door. You're welcome."

Journal Entry

A TRIP TO UPS

I pull up to UPS to run a quick errand. I'm seven months pregnant, and I have two dogs and one two-year-old in the car. "Quick" will have to be a relative term today.

I search through my bag for the set of keys that has the post office box key. I cannot find it. My two dogs start barking uncontrollably at the UPS man who is loading boxes nearby. I drop my car keys between the seat and the center console as I continue my search for the PO box key.

Then I recall my child playing with the PO box key ring at lunch. And I realize that the key ring is no longer in my possession as a result. The dogs continue to bark as if the UPS man were loading explosives. Into our car.

I open the sunroof to give the dogs some air while I'm in the store.

I grab the child out of the backseat and as usual she demands, "Walk!"

I put her down, and we walk inside. We get two steps inside and she takes off one of her shoes and points to the other, "Off. Hurt." I tell her she has to wear shoes inside and try to put the removed shoe back on. She wrestles away from me and takes off the remaining shoe. I give up fighting that battle and stand in line.

The child beelines for the candy display that is purposely placed at her eye level because the UPS Store owners are evil people who enjoy torturing parents. She starts to play with the candy. I stand in line and tell her to put back each candy bar she

➤

presents to me. (Note: The child has never even had a candy bar in her life. We as humans are just born with the instinct to pick up and demand all forms of chocolate, so I'm fighting against nature here, really.)

Meanwhile the dogs have not stopped barking. Now they've turned their yippee yaps to the poor elderly woman trying to get out of her car that she has unfortunately parked next to mine. The sunroof is open and yippee yaps carry very well, so the entire store is being subjected to their insanity, not just the poor elderly woman.

I get up to the front of the line just as my child has undertaken a very extensive candy reorganization project. I try to tell the Unamused Worker Man what I need, while simultaneously distracting the child into not being two years old. Both attempts are unsuccessful. I throw my certified mail at the man and go to get the child.

I grab the candy out of her hands and put it back in order, then grab her. She goes limp, in what is another born-in trait that every child in the history of civilization masters upon birth. She flops to the floor laughing, because this is all very amusing.

The poor elderly woman who just escaped my rabid dogs is now standing in line watching my child roll around on the floor. Knowing my child as well as I do, I simply say, "Fine, lie on the ground. I'll be over here when you're ready to get up."

I turn my attention back to Unamused Worker Man and complete my UPS experience. The child, not getting anywhere with her floor routine, gets up and comes to me. We walk out and I put her in the car.

I get in my seat and start looking for my keys. It is a good minute or so before I remember I dropped them between the seat and center console. I get back out of the car and lay my seven-months-pregnant ass on the floor of the backseat to look under my front seat for the keys. It is a nimble and attractive effort.

When I climb out of the backseat, the elderly woman is coming back to her car. My dogs greet her as an armed assailant.

"Your little girl is so cute."

I look around to see if perhaps she is speaking to someone else. She is not.

"Especially when she's lying on the floor, yes?" I ask.

The elderly woman pushes her walker to her car and shrugs. "That's to be expected. She really is a cutey."

God bless the grandmas.

"Take your time with the dessert menu. We aren't in any rush."

DINING OUT BEFORE KIDS

"We need to-go boxes."

"We haven't even ordered yet."

DINING OUT AFTER KIDS

*R*EMEMBER BACK BEFORE you had kids? (Take your time; I'll wait while you try to summon up the memory.) You'd get home from work and think, "I don't want to go through the effort of making dinner. Let's just go out to eat." Because back then, a restaurant was the *easy* eating option. Oh, what simple times those were for your taste buds. And your heart rate.

Then you had kids.

And all of a sudden a restaurant is no longer your happy place where the nice people bring you food and drinks that taste so much better than anything you could ever prepare (even their soda tastes better, with its bouncy bubbles of joy fresh from the fountain). Post-children, a restaurant is no longer Utopia; it's been transformed into a grueling challenge that must be survived.

All enter with the same hopes and dreams. ("Full bellies, clean clothes, no tears!") But very few exit unscathed. This undertaking is not for the weak or ill-prepared.

You have to come armed with the right equipment: snacks, toys, backup snacks, backup toys. You cannot *ever* let your guard down. Don't even *think* of glancing at that TV on the wall— that's when servers get hit with flying spoons.

Speaking of flying spoons (and flying toys and flying food): your reflexes are going to get a workout. You have to be quick and agile, ready for whatever comes your way. Because there will literally be things (namely food and utensils) coming your way (namely at your face), and lots of them. Items will be projected in all directions; the floor will be a wasteland of failed peace offerings you've made to the children in hopes of buying ten seconds of peace.

And speaking of servers: you need to know going in how they will work against you. They will leisurely allow you ample time to peruse the menu ("We've been here thirty-five seconds, we need to order now! There isn't much time!"). They will put food down *right in front* of the children (please see "flying food" section above). And they will not understand that once the Exit Plan has been engaged you are *done* and need to leave IMMEDIATELY. There is no time for idle chatter or talk of dessert. Hustle, people!

Once you leave the restaurant, the staff will have no idea that they've just witnessed an extraordinary test of physical and mental strength. But they will know that the table looks like someone left shortly after losing a wrestling match on it. And when looking at that table they'll be stumped as to how such a mess could remain *in addition* to the huge pile of dripping, sticky used napkins. We all wonder that. (In fact, I think I'll title my next parenting book *You're Gonna Need More Napkins.*)

Given its incredibly low success rate, you might be wondering why I even bother attempting the restaurant feat. But then you might be underestimating how much I dislike cooking. So I push on. With dreams of a peaceful dining experience somewhere in my future, I push on.

SURVIVING YOUR DINING-OUT ADVENTURES

I asked my MOFL for their advice on successful restaurant dining and whether or not it's something they do often. Or do at all. It seems some do, and distraction is the key to their success.

Sarah G., mom of four, said: "I had a small train set and track I used to carry in the diaper bag. The boys only got to play with it at a restaurant—that seemed to buy us an extra twenty minutes when they were small. Now that I have older kids, they tend to entertain their baby brother, so it has become a lot easier."

This is one of the only logical arguments I've heard for having more children. The more children you have, the more likely they are to entertain each other instead of throwing perfectly good bread rolls at the back of unsuspecting diners. Take note.

Carrie, who has two young boys, doesn't eat out much with the kids. "However, when we do eat out, I have some small things in my purse I break out once the supplied crayons and placemat lose their appeal."

Psychotherapist Katie Hurley recommends choosing kid-friendly restaurants and ordering for the kids right when you sit down. "Plan ahead (know the menu options), bring crayons and a coloring book, prepare the kids re: expectations (you have to sit in your seat, put your napkin in your lap, etc.) before you get there, and go early. You can't expect hungry little kids to eat and sit still on an adult schedule."

Karen, mom of one, had a great training ground for her restaurant lessons. "What really helped was the Disney Cruises we've been on. The waiters are so good with the kids, and I was able to teach Mikayla table manners in a 'nice' setting without the fear of being judged by everyone else. And they would come and take them to the kids club an hour into dinner."

(Do you think these waiters are available for hire?)

Brooke, mom of two, started taking both of her kids to restaurants when they were very little. "Usually to a restaurant that was not too nice, so if they cried or we had to leave it wasn't a big deal. We eat out several times a week and it's been more challenging with the boy than it ever was with our girl. We do limit any snacks before dinner to be sure they are hungry and will sit and eat."

Brooke hit on a couple of important points to note in the quest for restaurant victory: start young, and keep at it. Just like any other skill, proper dining etiquette won't happen overnight. I know it's really tempting to give up when you find yourself on a carpeted restaurant floor trying to sweep up the 95 percent of your child's food that he transformed into confetti. (By the way, you haven't lived until you've seen applesauce confetti.) But it's important to keep going back for more if you hate cooking as much as I do. Peaceful restaurant dining waits on the other side of that applesauce-covered carpet.

During our son's more difficult restaurant periods, we take a break from family dining; instead I try to take him out for a one-on-one date, so I can focus solely on him. I bring toys to entertain him. I order an appetizer and a drink, because let's not get ambitious about how long we are staying. I pay the bill before I eat. If he starts acting up I take him outside to talk about how

➤

big boys act in a restaurant. When his actions eventually make it known that he has no interest in being a big boy, we leave. It's tedious, but it's training hours logged and it's not disrupting an entire meal when the mission fails. If only a Disney Cruise waiter would come take him off my hands so I could eat my appetizer in peace.

But there is good news! Brooke reports that things will ease eventually. "Tonight was one of our first dinners out where we sat. Ordered. Ate. (At a normal people pace.) And we had not one, but two glasses of wine. Definitely a first time *ever* for that, so I think we are turning a corner in restaurant abilities."

So go forth, my diners! There is hope on the horizon! (And by hope, I mean wine, of course.)

FRENCH FRIES DON'T COME EASY

"Do you want to take the kids to Carl's Jr. for lunch?" my friend Michelle asks. You'd think that would be a simple question. And you'd be wrong. So very wrong.

I look at my two-and-a-half-year-old daughter, Vivian, who is running around the house with her three-year-old friend Enzo. The two of them are being careful not to knock over Michelle's ten-month-old son, Paxton. I look down at my five-month-old son, Daniel, who is happily watching the older kids as I hold him. I don't like the math here.

Anytime I have gone to a dining establishment since the arrival of the new baby, the adult-to-child ratio has been a manageable 1:1. Venturing out with a 1:2 scenario seems alarming at best, and CPS*-phone-call-inducing at worst.

But, you know, there are french fries at Carl's Jr. So maybe it will be worth the risk.

"Um, sure," I answer. And with that wholehearted decision we are off.

That decision is the first in a series of errors I will make that afternoon.

The second error becomes clear when I walk into the fast food restaurant and remember it is Saturday. And that every parent within a three-hour radius has decided to bring his/her children to Carl's Jr. for a weekend lunch. The sound is at a decibel that's hard to describe adequately. It sounds like—well, it sounds like

*Child Protective Services

---

every parent within a three-hour radius has decided to bring his/ her children to Carl's Jr. for a weekend lunch.

Note: I'm hearing impaired and can hear out of only one ear. That ear has a hearing aid. A hearing aid is essentially just a microphone in your ear. Most of the time this is a good thing, but in an environment like this the amount of noise coming into my head is nearly debilitating.

But we push on—the french fries are within reach now.

My friend orders her food and secures a booth with her two kids. I drop Vivian off at the table and stand in line with Daniel on my hip. By the time I get back, Vivian is lying facedown on the booth bench with her ass in the air, pouting over something. Enzo's food has already arrived, and Vivian is absolutely devastated that she doesn't have a toy like the one that came out of Enzo's kiddie meal. Of course it has made no difference that Enzo has shared some of his fries.

I kneel down next to her. While Vivian's brother flails his arms, trying to grab everything on the table to pull to their rightful place on the floor, I try to tell her that she has food and a toy coming too. But this is in vain: once she's in Pouting Formation, it is nearly impossible to talk her out of it. Looking back on it now, I realize that I should have just let her pout, because pouting is a quiet activity that involves no movement. And I probably should do my best to grab those moments when they present themselves.

But we have been working on appropriate restaurant behavior lately, and pouting with your ass in the air at the table doesn't quite make the cut. I am trying to build a whole person here, for goodness' sake. And that person needs to know how to act at a restaurant. Because that person has a mommy who really, *really* doesn't like to cook.

I give Vivian one more chance to change her position, but she doesn't budge. So I hand Daniel to Michelle and grab Vivian. She immediately goes limp and starts kicking. Of course. I take her outside, past the questioning looks of several fast food patrons. Once we get outside we have our Butt on the Seat chat, which has become a regular conversation outside restaurants lately. She agrees, through a few tears, to cooperate.

Back inside we have a good five minutes of relatively calm eating. I say "relatively" because the noise level is still scrambling my brain, and Daniel is still making it his life's work to pull everything off the table and onto the floor: forks, napkins, food, my sanity. I have a view of the kids' play area right next to our table, the one we've promised the kids can visit after they finish their meal. Every child I spot in the play area looks more diseased than the last. Coughing, snotting, covered in ketchup. The next week of my life flashes before my eyes: days full of two sick kids, our entire house brought to its knees by five minutes in an enclosed play structure.

I try to eat my salad with one hand while holding Daniel out of grabbing distance with my other arm. This is a unique lean in/hold out combo that makes for quite a comfortable eating experience. Vivian decides to stop eating and take off her shoes, because why not?

"Put your shoes back on, Vivian."

"I caaaan't put my shoes on."

"Put them back on now."

Then Daniel starts crying. Not that I can hear it over the noise. He is arching his back, trying to get free so he can rid the table of all that covers it.

"Vivian, eat your food, and put your shoes back on."

"I caaaan't eat my food." She pulls off her socks too.

A child in the play area with snot coming out of his nose pushes his face against the plastic window dividing us. And licks it. I'm suddenly overtaken with the need to put her shoes back on her feet. I reach down to the ground to pick them up, giving Daniel juuuust the proximity he needs to grab his holy grail: my plate. Now there is salad *and* shoes on the floor. And now I've lost it. I kick the plate in a flash of temper that, along with asses in the air, is a super classy thing to do in public.

I'm done.

"We are going. Now."

My friend, whose eyes are wide, says she is sorry. For suggesting the trip? For me thinking I have any control over my children? For the fact that I don't even get to enjoy my french fries? I don't know.

I pick up Vivian's shoes and put them in my purse. Then grab her, apologize for our mess and our behavior, and pull her out of the restaurant. We get outside and I bend down and tell Vivian she has to put on her shoes. We are about to walk through a parking lot. It isn't safe.

"I caaaan't put on my shoes."

I'm done with debating and am not strong enough to carry them both. So we walk through the parking lot with no shoes on. I'm going to win all the parenting awards.

We get to our SUV. "Look, Mommy, water on the ground, my feet will get wet."

"Yes, if only there was an invention of some sort that could protect your feet."

I open Vivian's door and have her climb in the car. I close the door. I go to the other side to buckle Daniel into his seat. He is screaming. I go back over to Vivian's side to strap her in. When I open the door she is leaning against it. It happens in slow motion, the falling. Yet, I still can't catch her. Her head hits the cement and I see it snap back. I'm convinced she has broken her neck. She starts screaming.

I drop to the ground and pull her into my arms. We are sitting in the water, on the cement. She is crying, "I fell in the water, Mommy!"

I'm still sure she has broken her neck. "I need you to move your arms. Flap them for me."

Now we are sitting in the middle of a McDonald's parking lot, crying, in the water, with the child flapping her arms. Daniel is providing a nice background music titled "Screaming Baby Trapped in His Car Seat."

The looks we are getting make me think CPS could be on their way at any moment.

I take deep breaths and try to talk myself out of leaving the children in the parking lot, walking down to the freeway, and hitchhiking my way to a new life. Or maybe just to a place where I can eat french fries in peace.

I'm too lazy to hitchhike, so instead I stand up and get in the car, holding my crying child in my lap in the front seat. I give her

➤

kisses on her forehead, I check for any major injury. I try to tell the baby to calm down. He does not. I start doing the breathing exercises I did while giving birth to each of them. I could use an epidural right now. Or three.

Eventually Vivian is well enough to get strapped into her chair and we head home. The drive home is eerily quiet. As if both children have received the memo that they may have officially broken their mother this time.

"Mommy?"

"Yes?"

"I'm hungry."

FLU SEASON ATTIRE

$\mathcal{K}$IDS, BEING JUST like real people, will get sick. This is the most unfortunate news a parent can hear. No one wants to see our little ones suffer. But more than that, no one wants to deal with the havoc a sick child can impose upon our lives.

Now granted, the fact that your kid will get sick probably doesn't fall under the "Sh!t No One Tells You" category of parenting surprises. But do consider yourself forewarned that the effect a tiny little cold will have on your life can be quite startling.

As your kids get older, germs lurk at every turn. Some studies say it's good to get kids out, to socialize them, maybe even attend preschool. I say all those studies are funded by the pharmaceutical and/or humidifier industry. In my independent studies, I've found a direct correlation between my kids being social and the amount of snot in my life. Is being a hermit really that bad?

There are also studies that say getting sick is helping my kids build immunity, so they will be able to fight off illness down the road. This makes sense, until I realize that the immunity I supposedly built as a kid is doing absolutely nothing to protect me from catching every sniffle my kids bring home. I'm so disappointed in you, science.

When I go into one of my kids' bedrooms in the morning and find a runny nose, everything starts moving in slow motion. I scream out, "Noooooooooo!" Then huddle in the corner of the room, not ready to take on the next two weeks of havoc this little runny nose will wreak on my life. Children will be sick, parents will be sick, grandparents will be sick, nannies will be sick, and dogs will be so happy that everyone is lying around doing nothing all day. All brought down by the abundance of snot in one child's nose during flu season.

Aaaah, flu season. An entire season devoted to phlegm. How festive. Before children, I hardly knew ye. Now the mere mention of flu season sends a shiver down my spine. I know it's out there lingering, and I know it will make its appearance in our house eventually, but when? I jump when I hear a sneeze and start loading up the children on vitamin C the second they say they are a little tired. "Are you regular tired or getting-sick tired? Do you feel clammy, cold, hot, stuffy?" I become a complete germaphobe. "You had a cold last week? Call me in a month and maybe we can hang out. Over Skype."

For some reason, every time one of my kids gets sick I start building an elaborate diagram in my head, trying to retrace our steps back to patient zero. As if knowing who infected him/her will somehow allow me to create a healing antidote, as in all of those pandemic movies where they are looking for the monkey. (It's a small possibility I will get a little dramatic when faced with sick children.)

If you are lucky enough to deal with a stomach flu, you'll soon realize that, between snot and vomit, all sick children do is produce liquids for you to clean up. Our worst experience with a stomach flu involved our poor little Vivi puking every ten minutes for five hours. What comes up after about three times? Colors. Fluorescent yellow and green mostly. Once colors started coming out of the kid, we went to the emergency room. And once the emergency room sees colors coming out of a kid, you tend to get in rather quickly.

Another bonus to having a sick kid is that a timer starts counting down the second you hear that first sneeze or are splattered with that first projectile vomit. At that point it is only a matter of time before you'll be sick as well. And that is when the real fun begins.

Trying to take care of a sick kid when you are not on top of your game is an extra-special slice of hell. The night after Vivian was in the emergency room with her stomach flu, we were back with my diabetic partner who was equally ill. It was a fantastic weekend overall. At a certain point we thought we should probably just move, so we could get away from the germs infesting our house. If I ever find the monkey who started that bug I'm going to have a few choice words.

Moms on the Front Lines

SICKNESS

I asked my Moms on the Front Lines for their tips on adequately preparing for the various Battles of Bodily Fluids. They agree that your best bet for not being completely thrown off the rails by even a tiny cold is to be prepared. Like a Boy Scout. A Boy Scout who works for the pharmaceutical and/or humidifier industry during flu season.

Chipper Jen is stocked up and ready. "I always keep chicken noodle soup, Tylenol, and powdered Pedialyte on hand. Also Pedialyte Freezer Pops. And of course wine for Mom!"

Sarah B., mom of two, recommends "Boogie Wipes and Tylenol."

For the massive amount of snot **Jenine**, mom of two, contends with, she uses more than tissues. "It is a disgusting idea, but the snot sucker is amazing. Clears the baby's nose and she sleeps!"

The snot sucker she refers to is the one you should have stolen from the hospital when you had your baby years ago. The ones you buy in the store are crap. If you didn't steal the snot sucker from the hospital, it may be worth getting pregnant again, just to snag a few. They are that handy.

Dana, mom of two, recommends another snot sucker called the NoseFrida. She says, "It's seriously amazing at sucking the snot out. I was scared to use it at first, but it's pretty awesome."

The reason she was scared initially is that the NoseFrida involves half the contraption in the kid's nose and the other half in your mouth. And that mouth of yours is doing the sucking. Good news, there is a small filter included in between your mouth and the snotty nose. Phew.

Dana also recommends: "Tip up their mattress so they don't sleep flat if they're stuffed up."

In preparation for a stomach flu, **Jenine** also makes sure she has on hand doubles of her children's favorite blanket or toy. "Waiting for the one special blanket or animal to be washed and dried because it got puked on sucks!"

Amy, mom of three, seconds that motion. "For vomiting, all I can suggest is doing a quick inventory to make sure you have plenty of clean jammies and blankies on hand . . . you can go through them very quickly!"

For colds Amy says, "Humidifier and Tylenol for sure. And I give myself permission to get nothing done until they're through the worst of it."

Amy makes a good point. The biggest thing to prepare yourself for is the screeching halt of any sort of schedule you have worked so hard to establish. Cancel the play dates, call in sick to work, and accept that nighttime is going to be a disaster. Hunker down behind your wall of Kleenex boxes, turn the TV on for three days straight, and wait for this storm to pass. It will seem like an endless storm, and if you have more than one child you'll be lucky enough to see the storm pass through the house like an infectious tornado.

In fact, you might want to pick up **Chipper Jen's** recommended wine in bulk while you're loading up on the tissues. Mommies need medicine too.

Journal Entry

MY FAVORITE SNOT FAUCETS

I have discovered, in my extensive and very scientific studies, that the best way to avoid your children getting sick is to never make a plan. Ever. If you make a plan months in advance you should probably make a doctor's appointment around that time too, because, you know—science.

It is 2:00 AM and I am up with my sick, snotty six-month-old baby boy. He and I have plans to drive two hours to visit several friends in the morning. I miss these friends and I've been looking forward to emerging back into the real world after the past half year spent in a newborn haze. But Baby Daniel and his stuffed-up nose aren't quite ready for the change in scenery, it would seem.

I'm up throughout the night with the sick baby and am overjoyed when the two-year-old wakes up with a runny nose as well. Now, instead of having a nice brunch with old friends, I will be spending the day tending to two sick kids. The words "snot faucets" are used to describe their faces, just to give you a glimpse into the glamour that is parenting.

We recently sold our house and the home inspector is coming by today. We need to be out of the house for at least an hour of his time. Which is extremely convenient considering the faucets of snot we are dealing with. The toddler doesn't want to leave, because leaving involves putting on shoes and a coat. Some people are born to rage against poverty or injustice. My little girl was put on this earth to fight the establishment's insistence on appropriate footwear and clothing. She has been called to the fight; there is nothing we can do to keep her down. Except, you know, literally hold her down.

I'm not sure that holding my squirming child down with my legs while dressing her with my arms was what I had in mind when I dreamt of the maternal closeness I'd experience as a parent. But here we are.

It's raining outside, so an easy trip to the park is out of the time-killing question. We end up in an empty pizza parlor. We have come armed with all our tricks: food for both children, toys, iPads, and crayons. These keep the kids happy for a while, but soon the snot takes over and the baby is fussy. I stand up with the baby on my hip, bouncing him in an effort to distract him. The two-year-old looks up as she is pulling off her shoes and sees me moving, hears music playing over the stereo, and says, "Dancing, Mommy?"

I smile and nod, motioning her over to me. Let's dance.

So here we are dancing in the middle of a pizza parlor, one of us with no shoes on. We are spinning, we are singing, we are moving to whatever beat we can find. And just like that, this has turned into one of my favorite days.

The day itself pretty much sums up parenting: lots of snot and tears, punctuated by little tiny moments of bliss.

THE SH!T NO ONE TELLS YOU

6

THIS CHILDHOOD WILL BE TELEVISED

Hello, camera phones

RAISING HUMBLE KIDS

"Mommy, that lady's phone is broken. There are no pictures of me on it."

THERE WAS THE Greatest Generation, the Baby Boomers, Hippies, Gen X, Gen Y, and so on. Every generation gets labeled somehow. I believe our children's generation will be bestowed the moniker Gen N, for Generation Narcissism. Never before has a generation of children been hurled through life with such a keen appreciation for their own image. This is not going to end well, I can tell you right now. Kim Kardashian will have nothing on this next generation.

Technology has reached a point where everyone has a phone, and every phone has a camera that shoots photos and videos. This means you'll not only have footage of every single moment of your kid's life; there's a good chance you'll have it from multiple angles. And instead of developing film and putting pictures in albums, we now just flip through the videos and pictures on our phones. At any moment children have hundreds of photos of themselves ready for perusal. Each one of those photos a wonderful building block toward constructing a very humble adult, I'm sure.

When my first baby was brand-new I had a *lot* of downtime with her. Between napping on me and nursing, there wasn't a lot of time for other activities. (That, and Mommy didn't have the energy for other activities.) With nothing better to do, I would play on my phone for hours on end, answering emails, checking Facebook, texting with abandon. Oh, and taking roughly 2,345,123 pictures every day. What can I say? She was cute.

I have three photos hanging on my wall that present photo-journalistic-quality storytelling: Pre-Yawn, Mid-Yawn, and Full-Yawn. I was taking so many photos I could literally flip through them one by one and animate them into a movie. Did I mention the downtime? Yeah, there was a little.

That was my child's introduction to her own image—and to exactly how enamored I was with that image. I somehow doubt her little infant brain could deduce that there was a small possibility the rest of the world didn't share my undying and somewhat biased opinion. All she knew and knows is that her mommies (and grandparents and aunts and uncles) think her image is just about the cutest thing they've ever seen. I can see this going well only when she goes into the world expecting all images everywhere to be of her.

Can you, and do you even want to, imagine an entire generation of children entering the world thinking that they are the center of it? And they'll have photo evidence to prove it. With the amount of videos/photos/Facebooking that will document our children's lives, each one of them will essentially be starring in his/her own reality show from Day 1. It'll sorta be like *The Truman Show*, but at the end our kids are going to be devastated to discover that no one has been watching.

While some kids will love the constant documenting of their lives, others, like my Vivian, will grow weary of the camera over time. Recently my stubborn toddler has refused to smile in photos. The child has the most beautiful smile: one that lights up her little face with joy. But the second I whip out my camera, her entire face drains of any and all expression. It's not even that she frowns, because that would at least be a little entertaining. Instead her face goes completely blank. And every picture looks like it could be used in a commercial to help save the children for thirty-five cents a day.

My phone is full of pictures of her emotionless face, or the back of her head as she runs away from me. These days the only way I can get her to participate in the documentary of her life is if I get in the photos with her. I put my face down next to hers, hold out the camera in front of us, and we compete to see who can make the craziest faces.

When I flip through these pictures on my phone, it's fun to see the two of us together, our relationship captured. Seeing them makes me sad that I've ducked out of most photos in the last few years, not wanting my tired face to be immortalized. When, in fact, the journey we've been on together is exactly the kind of thing that should be immortalized, warts and all.

Our impulse is to take five hundred million pictures of the adorable kids—rather than any of the dark circles under our eyes. But someday your kids will be tickled to see what you looked like back when they were little, and you, no matter how hard it is to believe it now, will one day look back at pictures of yourself and say, "Damn, I was young." These are the good ol' days you will speak of eventually, so try not to jump out of the frame of *every* shot. Also, maybe invest in Photoshop . . .

BABY BOOKS?

I asked my MOFL if, because of the digital age, they were, like me, heavy on cell phone pictures and light on actual baby books. Many agreed with my plight; few had any plans to do anything about it. Sorry, kids.

Chipper Jen agrees. "Baby book? No way! Everything is on my phone or computer! If either crashes I have no proof of having children!"

Heather, mom of three boys, said, "Yes, I have failed to make any of my boys a baby book. I think blaming it on the technological age sounds good to me."

Kaysee, mom of three, wrote, "I am so behind on my baby books. I figured maybe once they are all in school! Everything is on the phone and the computer. Every once in a while I just print out my favorites."

A couple of the (show-off) moms have gone a little further than us lazy women.

Monica, mom of four, had a fun idea for her photos. "The good ones I blow up and get printed on a vinyl banner and put up on the wall in the playroom. That's as close as you're getting to a scrapbook from me until I'm old and gray and have nothing to do but cry over my good old days. I'll put them in an album then. Maybe."

Overachieving mom **Jenine** said, "I was really concerned about this happening, so a few months ago I made big Shutterfly books for each calendar year. They are awesome and really reminded us of the first years. Of course it looks like Dad and I didn't start living until kids arrived, but they think that anyway, right?!"

All of the moms who share my baby book deficiency make me feel a lot better. At least my kid won't be the only one of her generation wondering where the hell her memories are. "Check the C: drive, honey. I think they're on there somewhere."

7

YOUR TV
HAS BEEN HIJACKED

By things with very high-pitched voices

Based on your VIEWING HISTORY your
very intelligent DVR recommends these programs:

Before Kids

**Travel
Show** **Gripping
Drama** **Intelligent
Documentary** **Raunchy
Comedy**

Based on your VIEWING HISTORY your
very intelligent DVR recommends these programs:

After Kids

**Alphabet
Fun** **Kid Songs to
Make Your
Ears Bleed** **Something to
Distract Kids
While Mom Naps** **Your TV Has
Given Up
on You**

$\mathcal{W}$ HEN I WAS a wee little lass, the majority of children's TV shows came in the form of Saturday morning cartoons. And since I was a champion sleeper-inner, even as a child, I never really caught any of them. Which meant my poor parents didn't have any choice but to actually engage with me in order to pass the time. (Alternatively, they could also encourage a nap, for which I was always game.) Imagine my delight over the years as I saw more and more TV stations dedicated solely to children's programming. I foresaw how easy my life would be when I had kids. The TV would do all the engaging for me, while I took a nap.

Unfortunately, and this was surprising to me considering her DNA, my child did not pop out of the womb with a remote control in hand, ready to stare blankly at the television for hours on end. Even so, when we heard that our cable provider offered a premium station geared specifically toward babies, we jumped all over it. I eagerly subscribed with visions of my fussy newborn instantly being calmed by the flickering of age-appropriate television. Shockingly, this didn't work out as well as I'd hoped.

First of all, newborns, with their underachieving vision, can't even see the TV—so for all she cared I could have been watching a *Godfather* marathon. Second, her attention span in the early days was such that she wasn't all that interested in doing anything for longer than about 3.8 seconds at a time. Which meant my hopes of her peacefully chillaxing through any TV (*especially* my *Godfather* marathon) were shot down before my finger even came off the POWER button. And we'll go ahead and look past "third of all" through "four hundred millionth of all": watching TV has been proven to make kids stupid. I was ignoring those "of alls" for the time being. (I'm not going to be able to afford Harvard tuition in eighteen years anyway.)

For those of you who don't subscribe to BabyFirst TV, I will paint you a little picture of what you're missing out on. Although it will be hard to truly capture its wonder in mere written form. Because the station is geared toward individuals who have the 3.8-second attention span I spoke of earlier, all of the programming on BabyFirst is extremely short. If you look at the program listings on their website—"The first site for little ones!"—you'll see that there can be up to seven "shows" in a thirty-minute period. This means they move through "shows" quickly, which is the first rule in holding our attention these days. The second rule is to confuse the hell out of people, so they continue watching in an attempt to grasp what is going on (think telenovelas). And this is where BabyFirst TV really shines.

What I love most about the programming choices on this station is the fact that those in charge have no interest whatsoever in making it appear as though there is any sort of theme or overall aesthetic guideline to their network. Shows vary greatly in look, execution, and quality. As I'm a graphic designer by trade, I find this all very jarring, but strangely hypnotic at the same time. I. Just. Can't. Look. Away.

For example, in a half-hour block of time you can hop from watching a phantom pair of hands slowly build an entire, very detailed scene out of clay (piece by squishy piece); to a God-like narrator tell the story of a little train engine (not animated) who lives on a farm (with real people) in what appears to be Ireland; to a baby sign signed over and over for four minutes straight; to a sequence with several overly enthusiastic adults who are way too excited about spending time with babies followed by a sequence with several babies who look like they are very confused by the overly enthusiastic adults; to a different pair of phantom hands drawing every detail of a picture (from first stroke to filling in the color); and to enough counting to get you through fourth-grade math (if fourth-grade math got up to only the number three—forty-two times in a row).

If that isn't random enough for you, wait until bedtime. At 8:00 PM, the little puppet bunny sings "Twinkle, Twinkle, Little Star," turns out his lights, and goes to bed. (You'd think it would be hard to sleep with a hand up your arse, but he seems fine.) And that's when the party really starts. If you know any tweakers, or would like to feel like one yourself, you need to tune in to the Nighttime Programs for Baby, because it will not disappoint.

BabyFirst TV knows their target demographic has trouble sleeping sometimes, so they do everything in their power to help. And if they can't get your baby to sleep, they will at least get the entire family into a deep hypnotic state that will last for at least eight hours. Score!

At night they keep up the frequent changing of programs, but the programs themselves slow down to a pace that makes you feel as if there might possibly be something wrong with your TV and/or brain. Some of the standout programs include a merry-go-round, just going-around, and around, and around; an underwater connect-the-dots that connects the dots as if it's moving against the tide; sand drawing, where they throw some sand on an illuminated table, and the phantom hands draw a picture in it; and a kaleidoscope drawing just moves innnnnn and oooooout, over and over again. At this point if you are watching with tweakers, their heads will explode and you'll need to seek immediate medical attention. However, good news: if you're watching with an infant, said child is probably completely ignoring the programming, even though the adults haven't blinked in forty-five minutes.

Eventually Vivian grew bored with Tweaker TV and we had to move on to shows with actual plots and dialogue. Since we've left Baby TV she has gone through many different shows—each becoming the center of her existence for an extended period of time. As soon as this shift happened, as soon as Vivian actually started paying attention to the TV and retaining what was being said, I started kicking myself for wasting so much time watching "baby-appropriate" TV.

Gone were the days of her blindly watching whatever program was on the television, or better yet, just ignoring the TV altogether while she played peacefully. Now she had opinions and taste in regard to what should be watched. It probably goes without saying: her taste was horrible. I will forever regret that I wasted my last few months of control over the remote by watching humans dressed in rat costumes singing in front of a green-screened outer space scene. Think of all the HGTV I could have been watching instead!

Vivian's first true love on the TV screen was *Dora the Explorer*. And it was a bit of an obsessive relationship. She wanted to watch *Dora* all the time; she asked for *Dora* day and night. I'd get her out of bed and her first word would be "*Dora?*" One time, when she was being especially adorable, I looked at her with all my motherly love, took her face in my hands, and said, "I love you so much, sweetie." She looked at me, saw an opening, tilted her head, and said, "I watch *Dora?*"

Methinks my child is not the first to have an unhealthy relationship with the Explorer, because that chick is on every piece of merchandising you can imagine. The geniuses over at Nickelodeon know the children are addicted, and they happily stock every aisle of every store with items to lure your addict away from the light. It's Dora's world—we are all just living in it.

Vivian even wanted to dress as Dora for Halloween, because: of course. The child, like Dora, has brown skin and brown hair. I tracked down orange pants, bought her a Dora backpack, a pink shirt, white shoes, and yellow socks, and got a Boots costume for her baby brother. Never has more effort gone into a costume that looked like I totally forgot it was Halloween and just sent my kid out with a bucket to trick-or-treat. "Look here! You're a cute monkey and you, um, are a cute little girl (sideways glance at horrible mother) . . ."

If you haven't seen the show, it's about a young girl with an abnormally large head (one that shrinks in size as the seasons go on) who goes on educational adventures with her pet monkey, Boots. I'm not quite sure why Dora's parents haven't been investigated by CPS for allowing her to venture to all corners of the earth with a monkey, but it's probably because they're too distracted at home counting all their merchandising money.

Dora also hangs out with a fox named Swiper, a kleptomaniac who regularly has to be told, "Swiper, no swiping!" To which he responds, "Oh, man!" And then he continues to be friends with Dora. Lessons abound. At the end of every episode Dora and Boots complete their challenge and sing a song: "We did it, we did it, *los hacimos!*" Just *once* I would like Dora to get to the end of her adventure and say, "You know what, kids? We didn't do it. Counting to ten and knowing your colors will not get you out of all of life's pickles. We did not *hacimos. Lo siento niños.*"

In all fairness to Miss Explorer, I do credit her for teaching Vivian her numbers, colors, letters, and shapes—in addition to how to deal with friends who steal your crap all the time. Dora does this by presenting a somewhat interactive show. She is constantly talking to the kids and asking them for responses. Unfortunately my child's brain gets sucked out through her eyeballs when watching TV, so Dora's calls for response end up being awkward moments when the animated hero is staring blankly for a few seconds at my kid, who is equally as blank. The only way I know for sure that the TV hasn't fritzed is that Dora is also awkwardly blinking while she waits for my child's brain to come back online.

Now that I think about it, this might be when she is sending subliminal messages to the children to buy toilet seats and Band-Aids with her face on them. Quite an entrepreneur, that one.

Moms on the Front Lines

TO TV OR NOT TO TV

When I posed the "Do you let your kids watch TV?" question to the MOFL group, the answer varied wildly from "No, I don't" to "I know I shouldn't."

Monica said, "My sister didn't let her daughter in the room where any TV was on for the first year of life. If I did that, my husband wouldn't know we had a baby."

Sarah G. said she didn't allow her kids to watch TV until they were two years old, "because research has linked ADD/ADHD to TV and brain development. It trains the brain to expect images to change every few seconds and encourages a short attention span."

Yes, everyone is well aware that television watching is generally thought to have a negative effect on kids. But, on the other hand, it is known for a fact that children running wild will have a negative effect on their parents. So then, there is a decision to be made. And there is a remote riiiiight over there. Calling out your name.

A lot of my MOFL mentioned using the TV as a way to occupy the kids so they can get stuff done. I will second that notion and say that TV can be a lifesaver when you are trying to keep a household functioning.

Kaysee, mom of three, finds that TV has a positive effect on her kids when they are getting a little too hyper. "Sometimes it is the only way to get all of them to relax." This is the case in my house too. When either or both of my kids are out of control, or perhaps on the verge of an epic meltdown, I will sometimes turn on the TV to head off a catastrophe and/or my desire to drop them at a fire station.

Like me, Kaysee has also discovered the joy of driving with a movie playing in the car. This is a recent addition to our travels, and has been a game-changer. My oldest has been entertained by iPad games on long car rides for a while, but baby brother hasn't mastered handheld devices just yet (unless you count as "mastering" his excellent throwing skills, which apparently he does).

This resulted in many a car ride with accompanying vocals provided by Daniel. He does not enjoy being strapped down, or being bored, and always wanted to make sure everyone else in the car was a partner in his pain. Since we got a car with a TV hanging from the ceiling, Daniel has been too hypnotized to realize he is miserable. And we've all been too peaceful to realize it's probably frying his brain.

Most of my moms also agree with me that there is some educational value in some of the shows our kids watch—thereby making us fantastic parents for allowing our children to stare blankly at flickering screens for hours.

Leah, mom of three, said that even some of the annoying songs that worm into your brain are worthwhile. "I like *Daniel Tiger!*" she shared. "It's a less creepy version of *Mr. Rogers* because it's animated. But they use little songs to teach great emotional concepts. My kids will sing them at appropriate times: 'When you feel like you wanna roar, take a deep breath and count to four.' 'When we do something new, let's talk about what we'll do.' 'When you're feeling frustrated, take a step back and ask for help.'" Apparently "frustrated" is a hard word to rhyme.

Salpy, with four spawn, has a compromise that includes a TV and occasional videos, but no cable. She also mentioned that without television her kids pass the time by playing with each other. This is a wild claim of actual human interaction in the digital age. I can neither confirm nor deny the validity of her statement.

While I do not question the anti-TV studies, I always go back to my own childhood and resulting adulthood as a measuring stick for how seriously to take the alarming "your children will become depressed, overweight sociopaths if you allow television in their youth" studies/warnings. My childhood was full of TV watching, and I mean full. I was a regular reader of *TV Guide* by the third grade. Television affected me in slightly different ways than studies have found. Instead of teaching my brain to expect images to change every few seconds, TV taught me that lying on the couch for hours at a time is fantastic. It also taught me that the DVR is the best invention of our time. (I actually had to *watch* commercials when I was younger—it was a trying time for all of us.) And if TV sped up my brain, I'm a little worried about exactly how slow it would be moving had I not watched TV.

So, will I let my kids stare blankly at a TV for hours on end, as I used to do? Probably not. Does that make me a better parent than my mother? Probably not. Although I will say that when she is babysitting the kids, I will occasionally enter the room to find my mom watching Fox News, at which point I get incensed. I don't need any studies to tell me that watching twenty-four-hour news stations is bad for seniors.

A POEM

- - - - - - - - - -

Oh sweet child of mine
With a smile so pure and a heart so kind

There will come a time, when you're old and grey
And you'll think back through all your days

There will be regrets my dear, at least a few
But there will be one for sure, I promise you

Forget love and friends, and all that crap
You'll think to yourself, "I should've taken more naps"

So instead of battling me every day of the week
How about, my dear, you just go the hell to sleep?

Love, Mommy

I READILY ADMIT THAT I am subpar at most of my attempts to parent in anything resembling an effective manner (See Chapter 1: You Suck at This). But nowhere is this suckage quite as painful as in my bedtime attempts. Well, not "my" bedtime attempts, as in attempting to get *myself* to bed, because I'm actually exceptional in that area. (I don't even need a bed; a somewhat quiet place will do.) But any and all attempts to get my children to sleep in an acceptable fashion (acceptable being fourteen hours a night as the good Lord intended) have been utter failures.

This is, of course, all my fault. I'm pretty strict with my kids throughout the day, but as soon as the sun goes down I'm a complete wimp. Like any other parental victories, getting a child to sleep well requires focus and a commitment to the long haul. Kids don't learn after one time of doing something, so as a parent you have to be willing to keep teaching them over and over again. I just don't have the energy for the long haul at night.

Brooke, one of my MOFL, has great advice: "Whatever your bedtime routine is, start it early. Like at four months old. Because once you start something it's *hard* to go back."

Because I didn't talk to Brooke before my kids became toddlers, I'm still struggling with getting them to sleep well.

When Vivian was still in her crib, we would lay her down and have to stay within eyesight in order for her to fall asleep. Then we would have to essentially army crawl out of the room and pray to the baby Jesus that the sound of the door shutting behind us wouldn't wake her up and start this charade all over again. There were nights when I just gave up and fell asleep on her floor. So as you can see, we have always been top-notch at laying down the law in the nighttime hours.

We've tried, at various times of frustration, to let either kid cry it out. The longest we've ever made it was five minutes outside a nursery door. Recently we were able to actually make Daniel cry it out, but we had to modify the technique a bit by having both of us standing near his crib rubbing his back and telling him it is okay. It was important that both of us were there, because if either of us was solo we would have snapped and picked up the child within twenty seconds of crying.

Karen, one of my MOFL, has no sympathy or patience for such things. "As a single mom I didn't have much wiggle room for long bedtime routines. I have things to do! It's all about consistency and letting them know who is boss. Two weeks of tears and hard work, and then the rest is cake."

In my defense, we do have a routine, and we don't vary from it much. On the other hand, at one point our bedtime routine was so long I began to think I might have to start waking Vivian up in the middle of the night so we could get a jump on the next night's bedtime routine. (Please see the "Bedtime Routine From Hell™" later in this chapter.)

MOFL Jill's kid was a master at delay tactics during their bedtime routine. "Our daughter was notorious for coming out of her room. *Every* night. *Multiple* times per night. She would come down to the landing and yell out, 'Mom? How do you spell armadillo?' Or, 'Hey mom. My vagina feels better!' She would do anything and everything to get out of going to sleep."

I do give her kid points for creativity, which is an excellent trait to see in a young child.

Honestly, although I'm exhausted, I don't worry too much about sleeping hiccups. When Vivian was little I would get myself so worked up over the thought that she would never sleep well. She needed us near her to fall asleep at any time of the day or night. Naptimes and bedtime were a collaborative effort that could take up a huge chunk of time. I'd spend that time in her room, staring at the walls and ceiling, wondering if I'd need to make sure they offer bunk beds in college so I can sleep near her.

Then, over time, she got better. She stopped freaking out every time she was left in her room alone, she started putting herself to sleep just fine, she stopped waking up several times a night just because she needed to see our faces. In other words, she grew up. Now, when Daniel has rough nights or wants to be rocked to sleep, I don't worry as much that he'll never sleep unassisted. I just go with it and remind myself that very rarely do people complain about how their teenagers hate to sleep.

Vivian is four years old and she still asks us to lie down next to her at night. And we still do. This sounds ridiculous, and it probably is. But the goal was to make sure she could fall asleep by herself, and she's able to do that, so I'm not as worried about the long-term implications of lying down with her at night. I guess I'm more worried about the implications if I don't lie down. I don't want to wake up in a few years and realize I spent all her little kid time trying to figure out ways to get away from her.

Whenever I find myself getting annoyed at night I always remind myself that this little kid is going to be a big kid in no time at all. And at that point she won't want me to snuggle with her or hold her hand to fall asleep. She'll be bratty and independent and horrified by my attempts at affection. So right now I'll take all the snuggles I can get.

I'll sleep when she's a teenager.

Moms on the Front Lines

TODDLER BEDS

I asked my MOFL when and why they switched their kids over to a toddler bed. We moved Vivian a little before her second birthday because she had a baby brother on the way in a few months, and he was going to be taking over her crib and her room. We didn't want her to realize the baby was kicking her out, so we instead made a huge deal about her new "big girl" room, which included a new bed. She loved her daybed, but started out sleeping on the trundle bed because it was closer to the ground. Almost two years later she's still sleeping on that damn trundle bed despite our pleas for a change in elevation. "But Mommy, all my stuffed animals sleep up there, that's their bed."

Sigh.

Karen moved her kid out of the crib when it became a safety issue. "I moved Mikayla to a big girl bed from the crib when I woke up in the middle of the night to her screaming and perched like a monkey on the upper corner of the crib. I want to say she was about two years old. The first two weeks during the transition I sat in a chair outside her room with the door closed. She would get up and walk out and I would pick her up and put her back, just like in the Supernanny show. The first time I would say 'goodnight' and put her down. The second time she did it I would just give her a kiss and put her back. After that I wouldn't do anything except put her back. For the first couple of weeks this took about one hour each night, but she's been a gem ever since."

Michelle had another baby on the way, so she tried to lure her toddler into staying put in his own bed. "We moved to a big boy bed when my oldest son was just over two years old. Since we had another baby on the way, we didn't want to convert the crib to a toddler bed. Instead we bought the coolest bed we could find, a car bed, so he would be excited to sleep in it and hopefully not climb out every two minutes."

Sarah B. wants to avoid all that nonsense and just keep her children in cribs indefinitely. "We moved Drew out of his crib when he was a month shy of four years old. We probably shouldn't have kept him in that long but he totally loved it and got in and out by himself. Owen turned two in August and we plan on keeping him in as long as possible. In the morning he calls for Drew if we don't go in right away and Drew gets him out! I think we have a great system. We may leave him in until he's a teenager!"

Brooke has a way to keep her girl from getting out of bed too early. "Sydney is pretty good, and we had her 'clock' to let her know when she could get out of bed in the morning. When the illuminated cow on the clock changes from asleep to awake, she can get up. We actually started using it when she was still in the crib to get her used to the system before we moved her."

Isn't all of this just ridiculous? The amount of hoops we have to jump through to get these little people to sleep? When all we want in this life is to lie down and rest? Oh, sweet irony.

In fact, I think I will go to college with them. And wake them up every morning at 6:30 with a bullhorn. Just to return the favor.

Journal Entry

THE BEDTIME ROUTINE FROM HELL™

I look at the clock. It's bedtime. In another life that would mean I go to bed. In the current incarnation of life it means I may see a pillow near my face in two hours. And the odds are that pillow will have cartoon characters on it. This life is exhausting.

We rally the children upstairs to begin the Bedtime Routine From Hell™. First, we must attempt a bath. The children are very willing to participate in the disrobing portion of the bath routine, but lose interest after that first step. On a good day we only have to chase the naked children around for as long as it takes the water to fill up the tub. This will not be a good day.

The kids take a bath in our big master bathtub. While the tub fills up, the kids remember that the master bedroom is their favorite room in the house and are so happy to be back in here after a rough twenty-four hours away. There are big beds to climb on, pillows to throw to the floor with abandon, couches to ascend in order to look out windows. All of this is, of course, made three bajillion times more entertaining because of the aforementioned nudity. I feel like if I jumped and ran around with no clothes on, it would be extremely painful (for both myself and anyone who happened to be within eyesight). But nothing is more entertaining to these kids.

It's time to get in the bath. The children have buried themselves under a pile of pillows. And they are no longer children; they are dogs and cats. And dogs and cats don't need baths. Duh.

The younger child is easier to catch, as his coordination doesn't allow for the quickest of getaways. Once he is procured and thrown into the water, we must begin our negotiation with the older child. She doesn't need a bath; she's not dirty. She is given two choices, bath or bed. She picks playing.

After 23,345 rounds of negotiation and an equal amount of tears, the girl is in the bath. She will be filing a report with CPS tomorrow.

Bath time is pleasant, until we actually have to clean the children. Especially the cleaning of the hair. I'm not sure Vivian would react any differently if I was pouring scalding, hot coffee on her head.

After the cleaning trauma, the kids are once again at peace and loving the bath, and it is so much fun and—well, now it's time to get out. They don't want to get out! They love the bath!! Duh.

We drain the water from the bath and each child gets lower and lower to keep submerged as long as possible. They are both lying on their stomachs as the last of their precious bathwater disappears. They can't believe how cold it is in here. If only someone would have taken them out of this bath sooner. This will be going in their CPS report as well.

Once out of the bath, the kids have little to no interest in putting any clothes on. They would be fine to be naked for the rest of their lives. Or, I guess, until being naked entered the "painful" phase that Mommy is currently in. After chasing them around I catch the youngest first, again. I wrestle him into his footy pajamas while he screams out as if I'm cutting his feet off.

It's easier to get the girl child into her "pajamas" because she has long ago decided that her "pajamas" are just underwear and socks. I long ago stopped caring what she wears *to* bed as long as she is *in* bed.

Now it's time to herd the children toward the TV room. Most experts agree that watching TV before bed is a no-no because, in addition to the negative effects TV causes in the daytime (stupidity etc.), watching TV before bed can stimulate kids' brains and make it more difficult for them to fall asleep. These experts have obviously not seen the way my kids go from spinning/jumping to blank stare/drooling when our nighttime TV comes on. It is a beautiful thing.

In addition to a little TV, this is time for a couple of little snacks. Vivian wants milk and water, as well as some crackers, fruit, raisins, salami, and maybe one animal cookie. Taco Bell's marketing of the FourthMeal has apparently been effective in this household. Daniel gets snacks as well, but just some Cheerios that he throws at the dogs. The dogs love TV time.

We have now reached about the halfway point in the Bedtime Routine From Hell™. For our efforts thus far the parents get a slight intermission to relax while the children stare blankly at the television. The parents could attempt a quick power nap at this time, but any such attempts will promptly be met with a child who is overcome with the need to climb an adult's body and sit on top of her head/shoulder area. Attempt any and all power naps with caution.

After TV time we move on to teeth brushing. Like all other activities that take place during the Bedtime Routine From Hell™, this one would have a higher success rate if there were some sort of lasso in the house.

I come back upstairs from putting the milk sippy cups in the fridge and I hear, "See, you are nowhere near the bathroom, you are hiding under your covers, and you, I can see you, you are right there in the corner. Just because your face is hidden doesn't mean I can't see you."

We divide and conquer, each of us grabbing a child and taking him/her to the bathroom. We work extremely hard to brush these damn teeth that are going to fall out of their heads anyway. Vivian spends fifteen minutes rinsing her mouth out, because she has recently discovered how fun it is to spit.

I am on Vivian Duty tonight, so everyone gives kisses goodnight and I enter into the most taxing part of the Bedtime Routine From Hell™. I am so tired, and there is a bed so close to me. In fact, I'm even sitting on the bed! It's sweet torture that I am not lying on it.

There simply cannot be lying on said bed until after there is first playing with every stuffed animal the child owns. Luckily the child has enough imagination and energy for the both of us, so I merely need to hold up a plush doggie or two while she enacts an elaborate stuffed animal stage show. The stage being the bed. Because why would anyone sleep on such a thing when you could have horses and monkeys and tigers playing hide-and-seek on it? That would be silly.

Following the stuffed animals' three-act play we must move all the animals. One. By. One. Off the bed. Do not try to sneak two at a time; that's a fool's game.

Now, it's time to read some books. Because reading makes children smart, while it drains all the life out of tired parents. Vivian's books go surprisingly fast tonight. She was gentle in her selection. She spares me the dreaded Wacky f'n Wednesday book tonight. I swear that book takes forty-five minutes to read. Also, she catches me on only three of my "turn four pages instead of one" tricks. "Mommy, you missed a page!" "Oh, I did? That's crazy! How does that keep happening?"

Finally, finally, finally, after the last book is read Vivian gets up and turns off her light. I give her kisses and tell her I love her. She pats the bed next to her. "Can you lay down with me, Mommy? For just a little bit?"

I am powerless against her sweet face. I fall down into bed next to her, rub her forehead, sing her goodnight song I wrote for her when she was a baby, and tell her I love her. She grabs my hand, holds on tight, closes her eyes, and says, "I love you too, Mommy." We both drift off to sleep.

Which is why the Bedtime Routine From Hell™ is my favorite part of any day.

9

YOU MAY START PLAYING BUNCO

Embrace the dice

TARGET MARKETING

BEFORE KIDS

AFTER KIDS

ONCE YOU HAVE kids it feels as if your life is officially over. That's mostly because your life *is* actually officially over. This means your days of after-work drinks, late-Saturday-night social events, and spontaneous get-togethers are probably shot as well. But people still need to socialize. That's why the moms that came before us invented Bunco.

Every month when I was little, my mom would get together with a bunch of other moms for a kid-free night of Bunco. They continue to do so today, as it's a great way to stay in touch. It would seem food, gossip, and prizes never really go out of style.

A few years ago I subbed at one of my mom's Bunco nights, eager to see what this wonderful game was all about. After my fourth plate of appetizers and fifteenth update on kids and grand-kids, I realized that Bunco night had very little to do with Bunco at all.

The game itself is like Yahtzee, but way less complicated, if you can imagine that. This detail is imperative, because the game cannot distract from the chatting. Men can get together and play card games that require thought, because their conversation needs are minimal at best. Women, on the other hand, and especially moms, need good conversation, life updates, and perhaps a piece of gossip to savor. Bunco fits that bill perfectly. You basically roll dice over and over again, moving from table to table, always concentrating on maximizing chatting and appetizer intake.

I was not yet a mother when I subbed at Bunco, so I didn't quite understand what was going on. Now that I have kids it has all become very clear. Amidst all the hustle and bustle of day-to-day life, work, school, naptimes, dinnertimes, and activities, your social life tends to take a backseat. Or isn't in the car at all, actually. Weeks and months go by without seeing your friends in person. If only there were a regularly scheduled event that you could put on a calendar and make part of your monthly planning. Your spouse or babysitter would be prepared for it, you would look forward to it, and it would force you to routinely take some kid-free time.

But what sort of event could you plan? A book club? That sounds like it would require homework. A party hosted by someone trying to sell you candles, kitchen supplies, jewelry, or sex toys? That sounds expensive. How about we buy some dice and cups and pretend to play a game while we really just eat and socialize? Sold!

If you are like me, Bunco holds an unfortunate connotation for you. The connotation being that only old people play Bunco, so how on Earth could you be involved with such a thing? I hate to break it to you, but you've procreated or by some other means come into possession of a child. After you have possession of a child, no matter what age you are, you are officially old. At the very least you are boring. It's best if you just accept this fact and don't fight it too much. Embrace the dice.

Life with kids and jobs and spouses can be a bit overwhelming and a lot suffocating at times. The thought of carving out time for something beyond your immediate responsibilities sounds difficult at best and like a strategic impossibility at worst. But I promise you it's worth the hassle.

As my youngest is getting older, we've finally started making it a priority for the adults to get out of the house, kid-free. Sometimes the adults go out together, but most of the time we go out alone. Maybe I'll go meet a friend for dinner, one that involves taking time for an appetizer before the entrée, and where there's no anxiety because the people I'm eating with won't decide at any moment to stand up on their chairs and throw bruschetta at another patron. Or maybe I'll just go shopping at Costco by myself and walk up and down every damn aisle at a leisurely pace, going back for seconds at the sample tables. I'm crazy like that. Whatever I do, even if it's only an hour away, I always feel a little refreshed when I get back to my kids.

Family psychotherapist Katie Hurley agrees that enjoying time away from your kids can make you a better, happier parent. "It's very difficult to be calm and present when you're feeling stressed, isolated, and/or depressed. It's the 'put the oxygen mask on yourself first' theory—if you take care of you, you will be better equipped to care for others."

I think I love that theory (mostly because it essentially equates parenting with being in a plane plummeting to Earth); it's one that so many moms, and women in general, struggle with. "I'll take care of myself when I have a little more time." But that time won't magically present itself unless you make yourself a priority. You can't wait for your kids or your spouse to give you permission to take care of yourself—you have to speak up and demand it. Sometimes, in order to be heard, you even have to demand it pretty loudly. But it is not your partner's responsibility to keep tabs on your mental well-being, and there's a good chance he or she does not know how much you need a little break. Try talking without the kids around. Make it known that it's a good idea for both of you to have some reboot time. The key is to think about this before you explode, having been quiet for too long. Explosions can be messy.

If this all sounds a bit overwhelming, keep in mind that taking care of yourself doesn't need to be a huge undertaking. Katie says, "A common misconception is that moms need to fit in hours of alone time to decompress—this can actually add extra pressure to young moms. They have to do everything *and* find time for hobbies?! Fifteen minutes alone in the bath can reset the soul as much as anything, and it doesn't cost a thing."

So sneak away from your kids once a week for some alone time. Be open and honest with your spouse about how suffocating this whole adventure can feel at times. And if you're invited to something with friends, join in, even if you are tired and would rather stay at home in your pajamas. If you are feeling isolated, or in need of some friend time, start your own Bunco night. If you want, call it Bunco Night to sound official—but really just throw out some Costco appetizers and wine, and forget the silly dice. Also, tell everyone to come in sweatpants—it could quickly become the most successful party you've ever thrown. I'm on my way.

Moms on the Front Lines

GETTING OUT OF THE HOUSE

I asked my MOFL if they take time consistently to do anything for themselves away from their kids. Some of them gave me blank stares.

"Does taking a shower count?" **Colleen** asked.

Brooke didn't think that counted in her case. "I'd say a shower but mine aren't regular enough."

Chipper Jen, not surprisingly, has always found time to be active. "Thursday night soccer with the girls! Also, I run. I have to. I'd go insane if I didn't. Stress relief!!"

A few of the other moms said they work out as well, and that it provides stress relief while doing their body some good. Most of them report working out early in the morning—which very well may be good for the body, but would be extremely detrimental to my soul.

Brooke pointed out that she's just recently been able to get back in the swing of taking time for herself. "I could never find a consistent time that worked well to work out. Now that the kids sleep all night I've been working out around 6:00 AM."

Brooke makes a good point: it can be really easy to fall into and stay in the same routine once you have kids. But as they get older it's important to be open to carving out a little time for yourself.

Sarah G., mom of four, has us all beat in the self-care department. "It's varied over the years: Bunco, Bible study, running, gym, yoga, girls' trips, date nights, etc. I found I needed more social outlets as a stay-at-home mom than I have working outside the home. I think I just craved adult interaction!"

And if you can't make it out for adult interaction on a regular basis, you can at least follow in **Chipper Jen's** footsteps. "I regularly pour a glass of wine for myself! That's something I'm consistent with!" Cheers to that.

10

YOU MAY NOT BE THE FAVORITE

And that might not be a bad thing

THE UPSIDE TO NOT BEING THE FAVORITE

I AM VERY CLOSE to my mom. I talk to her all the time, she lives nearby, and she's one of my favorite people. When I envisioned having kids of my own, I always assumed I would have a similar relationship with them. And naturally I assumed I would be their favorite parent. Or at least they would always run to me first, the way I always ran (and still run) to my mom first.

I'm not sure when Vivian started making her parent preference known, but I am sure I was devastated to learn I wasn't the Chosen One. It didn't make sense in my brain. I grew her *in my body*, nursed her for ten farkin' months (I got blisters *on my nipples* for this child), and spent more time with her than Becky did. And yet, I was still #2. (Sometimes, if my mom was over, I'd slip down to #3. Good times.)

I remember that I really started feeling Vivian's shift away from me when she was about eighteen months old and I was pregnant with Daniel. I'm not sure if that's actually when it started, but I do know that's when it started to break my heart. (This might have been influenced a teeny tiny bit by the crazy amount of hormones I had racing through my body.)

Most of the time the parent that is with the kids more becomes the favorite, but in our case it was the opposite. In our case I think Vivian enjoyed Becky more because for quite a while she was always the "yes" parent. The fun-and-games parent. Whereas I would spend all day disciplining Vivian, generally being the "no" parent. Becky would come home and very rarely back me up on my attempts to be strict. It doesn't take a genius to figure out why the child liked her more.

Also, pregnancy was hard on me. For the first five months I was gonna-puke-at-any-second nauseous all day, every day. If

I wasn't lying in bed I was desperately wishing I was. This is not fun for an eighteen-month-old. No longer could I run around with her, throw her in the air, or be game for an elaborate make-believe session. Even after my all-day morning sickness passed I was still absolutely exhausted all the time—so Becky stepped up into the fun role with gusto while I rested on the couch.

It was around this time Vivian started saying, "I no like Mommy!" on a pretty regular basis. And by "pretty regular" I mean "anytime I came near her." It's such a horrible feeling to be pushed away by your kid (sometimes *literally* pushed). It's like someone stabbing you in the heart. For me the most difficult thing was continuing to go back for more abuse.

In general, I don't care much what other people think of me. If someone doesn't like me, it's not in my nature to win him/her over so much as move on with my life and not give him/her a second thought. When Vivian was being such a shit to me, it took everything in my power to keep reminding myself that she was worth fighting for, and that I still had a chance to win her over.

Becky actually thought it was funny at the beginning, the ridiculousness of Vivian treating me as if I was coming after her with a chainsaw. But after more than one breakdown by her overly hormonal baby mama, Becky started to get the point that this was not funny to me. At all. We discussed it regularly and came up with a game plan that involved Becky telling Vivian it wasn't nice to say those things to Mommy, and that we love Mommy—even if she is a hormonal mess (and kind of a hard-ass).

Child psychologist Gail Marie Poverman-Kave has similar advice. "The most important strategy that parents need to employ is presenting a united front. Families should never fall victim to a 'divide and conquer' mentality."

I remember telling Becky in several conversations that I couldn't spend the next eighteen years of my life being the Bad Guy. It's not fun being the hard-ass, but we are raising people here, not trying to win the title of Homecoming Queen. So I think being strict is important. While Becky hasn't stopped being the "fun" parent, she has at least started backing me up when I lay down the law. And I will say that I have managed to loosen up a bit (a.k.a. I'm just too tired to put up a fight), which has also made things a lot easier.

I haven't talked to many moms who deal with this issue. Most moms I know are the favorite in their house, so they look at me rather blankly when I try to explain how difficult it can be not to be #1. It sounds almost petty when I'm saying it, as if I'm in junior high and the popular kids don't want to talk to me. (For the record, that's pretty difficult to deal with too.) On the rare occasion when I come across kindred spirits, I'm somewhat relieved to learn the issue was traumatizing for them as well.

I've spoken with two couples (one straight, one lesbian) who've dealt with a serious "favorite" issue. I was surprised to find that both had actually sought out a therapist to help them work through it with their partner. This made me feel great! Maybe it wasn't that I was just a hormonal mess when this was bothering me so much! I was so excited to know that other people were miserable too. You know, comradery, and all that.

Child psychologist Katie Hurley has good news for my comrades:

Although it can be frustrating when kids pick a favorite parent, there is some good news: playing favorites is a sign of cognitive and emotional growth. In playing favorites, your child is engaging on a deeper level and exploring relationships, asserting her independence (little kids are big on making choices), and even practicing decision-making skills.

In fact, playing around with separation points to several areas of growth. Putting all eggs in one basket (one other than yours, that is) is actually a sign that your child is secure in your parent-child attachment. Your child knows that you will be there no matter what.

Well, there you go. At least my heart is being broken for a good cause.

These days things have gotten a lot better, both between Vivian and me and between Becky and me. I make a point to spend one-on-one time with Vivian—to do fun things together, and take time for just the two of us—instead of trying to forge a relationship with her when her mama and little brother are pulling at our attention.

In the end, I know I'm a good mom. I've always known that. It's what I held on to when the love of my life wanted nothing to do with me. All I can do is continue being a good mom, continue giving her everything I have, and hope that at some point in her adult years she will be horrified when I show her the video of her kicking and screaming, "I no like Mommy!" I might also tell her about having to deliver her without the aid of an epidural, just to really make her feel like an ass.

PLAYING FAVORITES

I asked my MOFL if they had dealt with one parent being the favorite, and how they had worked through it. Not surprisingly, most were the favorite simply by virtue of being the mom. Also not surprisingly, this was not a huge issue in their household because their husbands weren't having sobbing fits over it.

Dana doesn't notice her kids picking one parent as the favorite every time. "I think that 'favorite' is relative given the situation. I am the favorite at bedtime, when they are sick, when we get ready in the morning, when they get dropped off at daycare or school, etc. I think I am just that comfortable security person for them. Justin is the favorite in the evenings after work because he plays with them nonstop instead of giving them something to pacify them while trying to make dinner (which I do). He basically gets to be the favorite for most of the fun things, but I am fine with that. I guess I feel lucky that there is a good balance in the family."

Sarah B. can sometimes feel the strain of being the favorite in her house. "I'm the favorite, which is wonderful until it's not. It's great to always be wanted and chosen. But sometimes I feel like they are sucking the life out of me. And I do get resentful that Cris is sitting on the couch watching TV while I'm putting both kids to bed for hours!! But I do love that I am the favorite, and I feel as if I have earned it by growing and feeding them for their first years!"

Sarah B. makes a point that I rarely give consideration to because it's not my reality: the fact that being the favorite can be a bit claustrophobic. I remember that for a while Vivian would only let Becky put her down for bed, and you might recall her bedtime is not a simple undertaking (please see Chapter 8: You May Be Too Tired to Sleep Train This Child). It would break my heart when Vivian shooed me out of her room, but on the other hand being able to veg out on the couch and watch a TV show helped me deal with my pain.

Only one of my MOFL had experience dealing with the same level of favoritism that we did. And it was just as scarring for her household.

Michaela, mom of one, told her story:

I went back to work full-time when Sam was about four and a half months, and was out of the house all day. Brad worked three days a week from home and he became what a friend referred to as the "lead parent." I just couldn't figure out my place or my role in our little family unit. On the weekends, if Sam needed anything, before I could even register what was happening in the moment, Brad was already doing whatever it was that needed to be done. He was just constantly hovering.

I wanted the chance to do the parenting stuff, the chance I perceived he was getting while I was at work, and the more Brad took over, the more I slipped into the background. He thought he was doing this to take stress/pressure off me, and had the very best of intentions. But I just wanted him to back off and give me a chance. So, there was always this tension, at least on my end. It was insanely hard on our relationship. I became quietly resentful, and felt isolated, rejected, helpless.

Finally, we went to a counselor. It wasn't long before she ferreted out what was really the source of our hardship: grief. That was huge for me, like, "Ohhhh, I'm sad . . . that's what this is." I mean, I don't know if I've ever been so sad, honestly—I didn't even recognize it as sadness. Anyway, it took us almost the entire school year to figure all of this out. Sam is still very attached to Brad, but I feel like I've learned to appreciate that as a stand-alone thing, not take it as a rejection.

If I have any advice for moms dealing with this issue, it's what Michaela has learned: don't take it personally. It is a well-chronicled fact that toddlers are a-holes. But don't give up on them just yet. I've worked hard to win over my a-hole without compromising the discipline I believe is important. I make one-on-one time a priority, plan fun activities to share with her, and make a point to be a little more fun in our everyday lives. All these things, along with time, have brought my little girl back to me.

Do you think taking her to Chuck E. Cheese and the park will help me stay close to her during her teenage years too? One can only hope.

11

YOU'RE TOO OLD
FOR THIS

And kids don't want to play with wisdom

KIDS

NOT EVEN ONE.

*P*EOPLE ARE WAITING longer and longer to have kids these days. Some babies don't make an appearance until their parents are in their mid-thirties—sometimes even into their forties. There are several reasons for this: longer life spans (why rush into the baby-making; we have plenty of time for such things), women focusing more on their careers than they have in the past (networking while wearing a BABYBJÖRN is difficult), and people getting hitched later (longer life spans, as above).

I was thirty-three years old when my daughter was born; my partner was thirty-six. Before the baby came along we had very, very comfortable lives. We had established careers that allowed us both to work from home, and we owned property, animals, and matching sets of plates. We had long since settled into official "adulthood." We had traveled the world, accomplished dreams, and could do what we wanted, when we wanted.

Because we made a decent living we had quite a bit of freedom when it came to our lifestyle. We ate out at nice restaurants a few times a week, we traveled on a whim, and we set our own work schedules. My work schedule was usually planned around my preferred sleeping schedule. (It's all about priorities, you know.) In short, it was a comfortable life.

Then we decided to have a baby.

And oh my goodness did that comfortable lifestyle come to a screeching halt.

All of a sudden our very loose lives became very rigid. Schedules became imperative. Cooking in the kitchen became required. Sleeping in became nonexistent. It's not as if this was all unexpected, but that doesn't mean it wasn't a shock to our very spoiled systems when it actually happened.

Now, keep in mind that we didn't even have real jobs before our first baby arrived. Yes, we worked and often worked long hours, but we set those hours ourselves. So we didn't even have the responsibilities or schedules of normal adults when it came to little things like working. Most days I wouldn't make it over to my office until noon or so, and I would usually be in my pajamas most of the day. Sometimes I would work until 2:00 or 3:00 AM, because I was a night owl (big focus on "was"). If work was slow, I would skip the office and go catch a movie or lunch with a friend.

Even our relationship was pretty relaxed. We spent most of our time together, but it wasn't odd for me to call and say I had made plans with a friend and wouldn't be home for dinner. One November Becky went with her friend to New York to see the Thanksgiving Day Parade, and I was fine with that. We both had lives outside each other and encouraged those lives to remain intact.

That all changed after the baby came along. I remember one day in particular when Becky sent me a message saying she had made a client appointment at 6:30 PM and would be home after the meeting was over. Before the baby this would have been no big deal, but since at the time I was holding a screaming infant, I was counting down the minutes until I'd have some help with this inconsolable child. I sent a message back that was along the lines of, "No you don't have an appointment at 6:30 PM, because you said you would be home at 5:00 PM to help with the baby."

That is when we realized that not only were we suddenly very bound to this child; we were also very bound to each other. And that was a very big adjustment to make. After that initial hiccup we set some ground rules, and now run all our appointments and plans past each other to make sure we always have the kid-watching covered.

Dealing with all these lifestyle changes was definitely the most difficult part of our transition into parenthood. I often thought that I was just too old for all this change. I had spent years settling into my comfortable lifestyle, and now it was all being upended by something that weighed six pounds. It can be rather difficult to teach old dogs new tricks. Especially when those tricks involve a change in sleeping pattern, turning on an oven, and adhering to a schedule. It was a lot to absorb.

Eventually our old lives slipped into the rear view and our new reality fully sank in. I've come to realize that life is a series of little vignettes: slices of time that can sometimes feel like completely different lifetimes. If you're lucky, like me, these slices can each hold tremendous adventures and lessons, dreams and relationships—all adding up to who you are supposed to be. Right now I am in my parenting slice of time. Besides the lack of sleep, it is by far my favorite time so far, but that doesn't mean it doesn't seem absolutely absurd compared to where and who I was just a few years ago.

A few years ago I spent most of my time alone. I made time for friends and family, but being alone in peace and quiet was definitely my happy place. Now, when I find myself in a particularly animated Mommy and Me class, I sometimes look around and honestly feel like I might be in a dream. One of the dreams I get after I take too much Nyquil before bed.

Back before I had kids it wouldn't be uncommon for me to get home, crash on the couch, and just watch TV for hours on end, or maybe just drift off to sleep at 7:00 PM if it had been a hard day. My dinner would consist of one of those premade bagged salads, or maybe I wouldn't have dinner at all, because who has the energy?

Now at the end of the day, we will fall down on the couch, the children gleefully running around playing and screaming. "Mommy, watch this!" (*Jumps three inches off the ground.*) "Mama, let's build a fort!" "Chase me!"

We will look at each other. One of us will say, "We have to feed them, right?"

"Yes, every day."

"Remember when we used to just go to bed if we were tired?"

"I don't want to remember."

"How is it possible that we are this tired? They're the ones running around."

"We are old."

"We *are* old."

I don't think I realized exactly how old I was until my children demonstrated how young and full of life they are. They always want more than I can physically give. One spin around leads to pleas for more spinning: "Why do you always skip right to the 'we all fall down' part, Mommy?" I get legitimately winded after pushing or chasing them a few laps around the house or backyard, and can feel various joints popping when I pick them up for the advanced acrobatics they love so much. "Mommy just dislocated her shoulder, sweetie. No more flying."

Often I guide my kids toward activities that will somehow involve me lying on the floor. "No, it's unseasonably cold outside for June, we don't want to run around, let's play Bury Mommy on the floor instead." I have handy pillows in their playroom so I can relax while they cook me food or play with trains.

At the same time, though, I feel as if the little balls of energy keep me young in so many ways. A few years ago I probably wouldn't have thought to spend an hour under a blanket with a flashlight, giggling. And that is actually pretty damn fun. Also, it was very rare that I would have a dance party in the middle of my living room, with people in their underwear and/or naked. I'd long since forgotten how much fun kites, Christmas lights, Play-Doh, rocks, and bouncing on the bed are. Every time I get to see my kids discover life's little marvels, it's as if I'm seeing them for the first time too. Watching their little eyes light up reminds me to find wonder in the world, if for no other reason than to be able to share it with them.

So, yes, I'm tired and achy and old. But I'd like to think that all the wandering I did before I had kids will make me better at being their mom. That the ways I pushed myself and the things I saw will help me in guiding them along their way. Because Lord knows, kids love playing with wisdom. "Let's put away those silly roller skates so Mommy can tell you about how to build a small business."

Moms on the Front Lines

ACCELERATED AGING

Sometimes it feels like not only did I start this parenting gig when I was too old, but this parenting gig is aging me at an alarming rate. My body has not withstood this task very well. My belly is constantly at about a three-months-pregnant size, I've discovered my first gray hairs, and my shoulder is always in pain from lugging ever-growing children around. I asked my MOFL if they feel the same.

Carrie is a mess. "I have three gray hairs that just appeared last week. I am always tired, and if I don't go to the chiropractor regularly I get headaches and back pain from being out of whack. I think I have aged twenty years in the last two."

Jodi has lost control of her face. "The crow has actually just landed on my face. I don't just have crow's feet wrinkles—I have the entire crow. On my face. Thanks to parenting."

I feel Jodi's pain when it comes to unfortunate reflection. Every morning I get up and look in the mirror, and every morning I'm genuinely surprised at the mom looking back at me. My eyes are bloodshot and ringed by dark circles, and the rest of my face isn't doing much better. I always think, "Damn, to look this crappy in the morning, I should have had a lot more fun last night."

My face looks like one of those "After" photos of how quickly meth can ruin a person's face. My poster will say, "Kids. Not even one."

Journal Entry

CHILDHOOD FUN = ADULT TORTURE

I don't think I was quite prepared for how much jumping I would do as a parent. Between bounce houses, music class dancing, and gymnastics, I feel like this parenting thing is similar to boot camp in the physical activity required.

At a recent birthday party for a young child, I realized that a kid's birthday party is not complete if the parents aren't sweating profusely. "Yes, honey, I will climb up that thirty-foot-tall inflated slide thing while holding you. That does sound like a celebration and not at all like an emergency rescue drill."

Nothing makes you feel the profound shift in your life quite like trying to carry on a conversation with another adult while you are both "sitting" in a bounce house with various limbs flying all around you. You push on with the conversation even though it is nearly impossible to hear the other person over the soul-crushingly loud noise level required for optimal birthday fun. You know you've reached an expert level of parenting abilities when your conversation doesn't stop at all as kids and balls bounce off you.

I'll admit even I am guilty of torturing parents in the name of celebrating my child's birth. We went to a play-structure-type place for Vivian's second birthday. It was a huge contraption that would have been perfect if the kids were about five years old. Children could run themselves ragged while parents lounged around and talked. But instead I thought it was a good idea to invite twenty toddlers to this human-sized rat maze. Each parent gave me a more menacing look than the last as I passed them in the cage. We were all hunched over, trying to keep up with our crazed children, sweating from the maze's extreme lack of ventilation. I knew cake and pizza were not going to be a big enough reward for enduring this "fun."

I feel like my life is full of things that are considered fun to my children and could also possibly be used to torture prisoners for heinous crimes and/or get them to give up any and all secrets they may be harboring. For instance, I used to be a well-respected professional woman, and now I go to Mommy and Me music classes. My absolutely favorite part of music class is when the teacher takes out a small tuning instrument and blows into it to make sure we are on juuuust the right note before starting our humming and hand movements with the children, who are picking their noses and rolling around on the ground farting. If only all education remained this simple, I would have gotten four PhDs.

This class is intended to introduce children to the joy of music and feed their little brains with intelligence-building songs and dance. It does this by mostly having the children bang pots and pans while watching their formerly respected parents dance around them with scarves. It's a scene similar to one you find on the beach near bonfires after adults have ingested large quantities of alcohol and drugs.

If only music class had an open bar.

12

TODDLERS DON'T EAT
Don't even bother trying to feed them

FOOD PRESENTED TO TODDLER

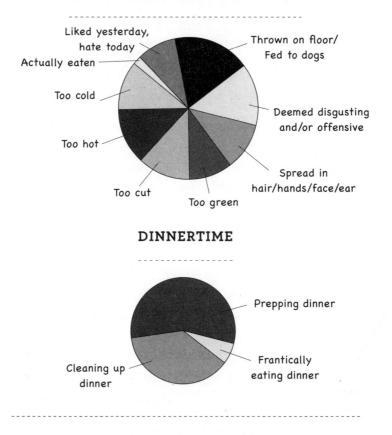

Liked yesterday, hate today

Actually eaten

Too cold

Too hot

Too cut

Too green

Thrown on floor/ Fed to dogs

Deemed disgusting and/or offensive

Spread in hair/hands/face/ear

DINNERTIME

Prepping dinner

Frantically eating dinner

Cleaning up dinner

I HAD KIDS WITHOUT putting nearly enough consideration into the fact that I would be responsible for feeding them several times a day. This was poor planning, to say the least.

If you are anything like me, you were very disappointed that your children didn't arrive with easy-to-follow recipes and/or awaken in you the desire/ability to cook. There are some days when I look at them and say, "Good Lord, how is it time to feed you again? I haven't even cleaned the table from our last attempt at a meal."

I breastfed both kids, Vivian for ten months and Daniel for thirteen months (though the boy would have preferred to never give up his boobs). Breastfeeding always felt like such a pain to me, because it required my boobs (and everything else attached to them) to be present in order for the children to eat. This was especially true for sweet Daniel, who would not take a bottle until he was eight months old. I would bitch and moan about the things I couldn't eat or drink while breastfeeding and about having to be available every three hours to nurse the child. Then, once the kids started eating food that wasn't being produced by my body, I realized with some dismay how great breastfeeding had been.

Today, I would be so damn excited to just whip out my boob three times a day instead of trying to figure out what the hell to present these children. I say "present" because that's all I'm really doing: presenting the food for their approval. Unfortunately, the food I present is usually met with varying degrees of disapproval. Those degrees range from a polite "No, thank you" to chucking it across the room because only a dog would eat such a thing (the dogs will gladly eat all such things). How dare I be so presumptuous as to guess what their picky palates want today? "And who on Earth told you to cut that thing in half?! Get it out of my sight immediately and try again, large human."

I've come to realize that eating, like all other things toddler, is about control. Toddlers are just entering into this time of exploring their independence, and they are ever so frustrated to constantly be bumping up against a large human who is exploring various ways to say no. This is when they start to realize that parents are in their lives primarily to be a buzzkill for the next eighteen to forty-five years.

Toddlers really really want control, and unfortunately for them, they have control over very little in their lives. Unfortunately for parents, the two areas where they *do* have a little control concern how and when food goes in and out of their bodies (please see Chapter 20: Potty Training Is the Sh!ts). Which is why mealtime can become such a tremendous pain in the ass.

I always try to make my parenting decisions based on what is best for the long-term development of the child, not just what is best for my sanity in any given second. This means taking the tough road sometimes and butting heads with a child I am attempting to mold into a functional human. But when it comes to food, I've stopped thinking of it as a huge long-term undertaking. This is not to say I let the kid eat french fries and doughnuts for every meal because that's what she wants (who doesn't want that, really?). But I also don't worry too much about the kids having overly adult or adventurous palates right now.

My kids are always offered whatever the adults are eating, but generally they end up eating one of their four or five go-to meal choices. Everything else about their lives is a big comforting routine—why wouldn't their food choices be too? I've had *Finding Nemo* on a loop in my car for the past six months; what makes me think these kids are super excited to experiment with new things?

The only thing I've made a point to enforce from an early age is the consumption of fruits and vegetables. It is one of my biggest accomplishments to date that my kids think broccoli and cauliflower ("white broccoli") taste good. I've put aside my dislike of all vegetables and made a point to introduce the kids to the green early and often. I wasn't introduced to vegetables as a kid, and they are the only food I still turn my nose up at as an adult (because they are gross). But other than that, I don't worry too much about whatever weird phases they're going through, because they always work out to be just that, a phase.

You've decided you don't like cheese in cubed or shredded form but do enjoy quesadillas and pizza? Fantastic. You need to shake the saltshaker over your tomatoes before you eat them, even though there's not actually any salt in the saltshaker? Here ya go. You will only accept a plate with three or five pieces of meat, and may break into sobs if there is any other number? Great: we're working on counting *and* getting protein! So many birds with the one stone. Speaking of birds, it's totally fine that you've decided you don't like eggs in absolutely any form whatsoever, even though you've never tasted any form whatsoever. Sounds like solid logic to me; carry on.

Child psychologist Gail Marie Poverman-Kave agrees that toddlers might not be ready for a wide assortment of foods. "Most toddlers are what we would refer to as 'picky eaters.' They are, in fact, just different eaters than we are for some very specific reasons over which we and they have no control. First of all, their taste buds are not fully developed. Taste buds change as we get older. Children's taste buds will change—we just need to be patient and make sure that we don't turn eating into a power struggle. We don't want to create eating disorders later in life."

Avoiding a power struggle is my main goal during mealtimes. If they sense a struggle, they will refuse to eat just to prove a point. But even without a battle, there are some days when the kids don't seem to eat at all. Sometimes I think my kids might be doing research for their revolutionary new diet plan: "Eat Every Third Day to Keep Your Toddler Figure." It can feel like I present them with a variety of food, hoping that one will strike their fancy, and all they do is take two bites of yogurt before they say, "All done!"

This used to frustrate me to no end. You have to eat! I think it's a law that I have to feed you! But then the next day the same kids will have what I refer to as an Eating Day. On an Eating Day one or both of the children seem to do nothing but eat all day. They clear their plates one, two, three times. They cannot be stopped—they are storing up for winter.

Eventually I stopped worrying so much about how much they ate, because they are humans, I have food to offer them, and when they are hungry they will eat. There are some times when I don't feel like eating a lot; I'm not sure why I would expect their bellies to be any different. I don't even do the "Eat one more bite of that, and then you can get up" thing. Because if they wanted to eat another bite, they would have. And if I were full and someone told me I needed to eat another bite before I could leave the table, I'd probably throw the food at him/her too. (My dogs would be super excited that the adults were joining in on the food-throwing.)

My only sticking point with this general laissez-faire mealtime routine is that sometimes my stubborn toddler is not eating simply for some stubborn reason. Maybe a butterfly fluttered its wings outside and set her off, or something equally as life altering. And now she's not going to eat, because butterflies are the worst. Some would say, let her starve, to teach her a lesson.

Child psychologist Katie Hurley disagrees with this strategy. "Some people argue that putting kids to bed hungry teaches them an important lesson. Toddlers aren't actually developmentally capable of learning that lesson just yet, so putting them to bed hungry could mean a middle-of-the-night temper tantrum or a really bad (and early) morning the next day."

In Vivian's case you could almost set a "timer to terror" as soon as she refuses to eat. If she goes without food for too long, the entire neighborhood will have to hear about it. So saying, "Fine, don't eat! Starve, for all I care!" doesn't work so well. Because in about thirty minutes she will make very sure I care that her low blood sugar has kicked in and we are all left trembling in a corner seeking to avoid her wrath.

When we're in this situation I move into Just Eat mode. I still don't offer the french fries and doughnuts (but, seriously, how good is *that* sounding right now?), but I will offer her something from the pantry that I know she'll eat. Maybe some crackers or a fruit squeeze snack. A lot of times if I offer a little snack and defuse the situation a bit, she will forget she was angry about the butterfly and relax into mealtime as normal.

Katie Hurley has tips for avoiding this power struggle. "Put several small bites of foods on the plate. Some of it should be the family dinner, some of it can be the safety food to fill them up. Instead of stressing about how much they're eating or what they're eating, try to make it fun."

So you know, if all else fails you could just do some jousting like at that Medieval Times restaurant, or maybe put on a mouse costume like Chuck E. Cheese. To make it fun. You know what sounds fun to me? A meal without any of my table mates whizzing a banana past my head and/or standing up on their chairs declaring, "All done!" Also, I could go for some fries and a doughnut.

Moms on the Front Lines

EAT!

I asked my MOFL how they corral their children into eating every day. I also asked for any tips they had for dealing with picky eaters (a.k.a. toddlers).

Sarah G. has four kids and no time to be a short-order cook. "We don't make food too big a deal: eat what's served or don't eat, I don't really care, I'm just not making any substitutions. I've never adopted the 'kid food' mentality. Meaning, for dinner I make one meal. I'm not cooking a meal for the adults and something different for kids."

Child psychologist Gail Marie Poverman-Kave has some ideas for expanding your menu a bit. "If your child likes chicken fingers, try grilling them instead of serving the breaded ones. If your child will eat a plain hamburger, try meatloaf that is not spicy. There are some books out there that teach parents how to 'sneak' fruits and vegetables into their children's diets, but I fear that this further serves to perpetuate the idea that healthy foods aren't fun or can't possibly taste good."

Michelle lets her kids get involved in the cooking. "When my kids are being picky, I let them help me choose something healthy for dinner and help me cook it. They are always more likely to eat something if they have helped prepare it. They can help cut with a butter knife, use measuring cups, and stir ingredients. It might get a little messy, but they are always willing to try their creation."

Chipper Jen's kids have to keep looking at the same damn meal until they eat it. "My rule is, they don't have to eat their meal. But if they choose not to eat it and they get hungry later, that is what they get to eat (no alternative snacks, etc.)."

Deanna has had about enough of her kids' changing taste buds. "Our biggest problem has always been how inconsistent the kids' eating habits are! They love spaghetti one night and then the next week they don't like it anymore. It is *so* frustrating. Especially since there is no rhyme or reason to why they've changed their minds. I love to cook and it has made me hate making dinner on many occasions."

The good news for me is that I've never loved to cook or even been very good at it. So my kids haven't taken away any joy in that area of my life. In fact, they've probably added years to my life by forcing me off my previous french fries/doughnut diet. And even despite my sleep deprivation, my reflexes are at an all-time high from years of meals spent with one eye on the lookout for flying objects and/or falling milk cups and silverware. So it hasn't all been bad. Who knows, maybe I'll get bored once the kids actually start eating like respectable humans. Where's the fun in that? I know for certain the dogs are going to be heartbroken.

13

PICTURES ARE DECEIVING

"Smile for the camera!
We are happy, dammit!"

Mom's effort to get a good photo.

Resulting photo.

$\mathcal{S}$OMETIMES I FEEL I should start a movement wherein everyone posts only true-to-life photos on the various social media feeds for one day. It would be so damn liberating. We could all come together and admit that for every good photo we post of our kids or family, there are 328 photos that look like they belong in a CPS file. We could also discuss how many calories we all burned while trying to get the children to smile during our photo shoots. The dancing and jumping and waving of arms required to capture a "natural" photo of children rival any workout routine you'll ever see on *The Biggest Loser*.

One of my favorite things to do is ask moms about what went into getting the perfect shot they posted on Facebook. The stories always tickle me so. And moms love telling me all about their hellish experiences, as if they've been dying to let the truth fly free.

They have tales of wrestling children into matching outfits ("Yes, we need to wear these outfits you've never worn in your life so that our pictures accurately reflect this time in our lives"), styling hair juuuuuust right ("Do not even think about moving your head until after this photo shoot—we are going for the natural look"), then racing against the tantrum clock to try to snap as many photos as you can before you lose one or all the children to the dark side ("It took three hours to get us put together enough to take photos, and about three minutes for us to all fall apart").

I have only two children and will not be having any more, mainly because I can't imagine ever capturing a decent family photo with more than two kids. Every child you add to the family decreases your chances of ever getting even one photo of all of you smiling during their childhood. There's always going to be at least one kid who ends up ruining every photo by looking as if he/she is plotting the demise of everyone involved in this photo-shoot charade. Frame it!

I asked my MOFL about their photo attempts. Dana, mom of two photogenic kids, has the math figured out: "In general, for every 'good' picture I get of one or both of my kids, I feel like I take about twenty-five 'bad' ones. It's a numbers game. If you take thirty, you are bound to get one good one in the bunch!"

Jen pulls out all the stops to capture her special moments. "I despise taking pictures. This year I had to bribe my son to wear something besides Nike warm-up pants and a jersey (even with the bribe he still had a total crying fit that made us even later than normal to pictures). Then I had to have two separate candy bags, and I literally fed my kids like birds to get them to sit next to each other and pretend to like each other for thirty seconds. End result: one or two amazing pictures with a little help from Photoshop! The end! Whew!"

Journal Entry

FA LA LA FRIGGIN' LA

It's the day after Thanksgiving and therefore the holidays are officially happening. Bring on the cheer and chocolate. Now that Daniel is getting a little bigger, we will try to reinstate our family tradition of going to cut down a Christmas tree. Last year the thought of involving a six-month-old in our Paul Bunyan adventure sounded like a good way for someone to lose a limb or at least some sanity. The year before that I was pregnant, and my all-day morning sickness made any drive farther than one mile out of the question, so down to the local parking lot we went to "cut" our tree.

This year, however, I'm not puking, Daniel is walking, and all signs point to holiday cheer just up into the mountains a bit. It's going to be fantastic. I will bring my fancy camera and take photos of the children frolicking amongst Christmas trees and other natural wonders, and I will have my Adorable Christmas Card Photo done in November! Oh my goodness, this will be festive!

About five minutes into our drive, Daniel has had enough of the holidays. His sister is peacefully playing on her iPad and would be happy driving to Canada as long as she had battery power. Daniel, on the other hand, does not enjoy going more than 3.2 seconds without moving, climbing, crawling, or jumping on something. Being restrained in a car seat is his version of hell. So he decides to scream at the top of his lungs, which is everyone else's version of hell. So far, all the festive is hurting my ears.

We try to give him one of our phones, so he can watch a video while we drive. This works for about four seconds, until he gets so excited about the video that he starts to touch the screen. Which stops the video. I hate you, Apple. Then he gets mad and throws the phone. Screaming resumes. Becky tries holding the phone in front of him so that he can watch but not touch the phone. He then wants nothing more in this life than to hold the phone, to just touch it one last time. Meanwhile the screaming has reached whole new octaves.

Our car of jolly finally reaches the Middle of Nowhere Christmas Tree Farm, which is quaint and isolated and in nature and—wait, there's a line of forty-two cars waiting to get into the farm! Apparently we are not the only ones out on the day after Thanksgiving, looking for serenity amongst the trees (which are all going to be slaughtered and made to wear blinking lights at their funerals).

The line of forty-two cars is not moving. Daniel is not amused.

I tell Becky to go up to the front and figure out what is going on. The fact that we are waiting in the middle of a bunch of trees to get to another bunch of trees is more than a little frustrating. Becky makes the hike past the other cars, then comes back. "They only have a little bit of parking, so we have to wait until some people leave, so we can park."

Maybe this year they could have people chop down the trees all around the parking area, then lay some cement down and build a proper parking lot. So there is more room for us all to enjoy the serenity and isolation of nature.

After an excruciatingly long fifteen-minute wait, we finally get into the parking area, then get out of the car and make our way to another line of people waiting to be taken by truck to the trees. We are surrounded by trees during this wait. Daniel has been walking for about five months and has no interest in being held, because the world is his to explore. He does most of his exploring with his forehead, as is evident by the huge bruise and unicorn-looking lump he is sporting today.

Being out in an unrestricted space nearly causes his brain to explode with excitement. He is overwhelmed by the amount

➤

of things around us that he has yet to bump his head on. It's important that he not waste any more time doing things like standing in orderly lines. I chase Daniel around, attempting to corral him into not being a toddler. I'm holding the huge tree-cutting saw they give everyone. It's an image that childhood memories are made of.

We finally load into a pickup truck and drive up into the mountains to be with nature, and then to destroy it. For the sake of holiday cheer. Once we get to the unsuspecting trees, I decide that this will be where the Adorable Christmas Card Photo will be taken. Unfortunately, the kids are not on board with the Adorable requirement.

They won't stand near each other. Daniel has found a stick he is waving in the air/at his sister. His sister is crying because she is being attacked by her brother. Becky is behind me jumping, singing, waving her arms around, and calling out their names in an attempt to get them to look even a little bit Adorable for just the split second required for a photo. This is too high a requirement for my children. They will not be giving up any split seconds.

Daniel has his sights on discovering the entire forest. Vivian would like to examine every fallen pine needle by picking them up one by one. Becky starts offering any and all bribes she can think of. The children are unbribable. I give up. Let's go cut a friggin' tree.

There is a flat area just a little bit ahead of us on the left, full of lovely trees. So Becky heads to the right, up a steep dried creek bed. There are no easily accessible trees in the creek bed. But she thinks she sees some a short hike up a hill. Because hikes up a hill with toddlers are always a good idea.

I follow behind Daniel as he walks/falls along the very uneven creek bed. I reach out to catch him when he falls, trying to avoid a head injury. Becky and Vivian are quite a bit ahead of us, because they have been walking for more than five months. And Vivian is smart enough to let Mama carry her when the hiking gets too tough. (My DNA presents itself in the most subtle ways.) Meanwhile, Daniel is hitting my hand away every time I offer it for support.

Becky finally stops and points up to a tree that is about fifty feet up a steep hill. "Do you like that one?"

I look up at the hill. "If it can make this be over, then yes, I love it. You know there are trees over there, where it's flat?"

Becky throws her bag down, grabs the saw, and starts climbing the hill. Alrighty.

I decide to attempt another photoshoot. I sit Vivian down in the dried creek bed and hand her a rock. I lure Daniel over with a very exciting stick. He comes over because a stick has the potential to hurt him as badly as walking does, so it's worth his attention. Instead of having an ocean of Christmas trees as their backdrop, I instead have them sitting in a dried creek bed, surrounded by rocks and dirt. It's fine. I'll Photoshop them somewhere festive later.

After slipping and falling several times in her climb up to it, Becky has finally made it to The Tree. She is trying to figure out a way to saw down a tree when she needs to hold on to the tree in order to stay balanced on the steep hill. I know better than to make any suggestions.

I go back to the kids, who are now fighting over Daniel's stick. Daniel is crying, Vivian is pouting. I start taking pictures. Becky is sawing the tree. It is so steep that she is above the tree on the hill, with her feet on the trunk to keep gravity from taking over. It's nearly impossible to saw the trunk of the tree without getting pummeled in the face with tree branches.

The kids are still crying.

Becky is struggling. She cuts through about two thirds of the trunk and she is out of energy. So she just starts kicking the tree with one foot. The other foot is still on the trunk, barely keeping her balanced. There are people watching her from atop the hill she is on. They are laughing. She finally gets the tree to "timber!" and it tumbles down the hill. She slides back down the hill, holds up the tree to show the kids, and smiles. Vivian starts crying hysterically.

I look at Becky to see that her lip is fat, her teeth covered in blood. She managed to strike herself in the face with the saw while chopping down the tree. Vivian is traumatized by the amount of blood, and rightfully so.

Because of the trauma both children have lost the use of their legs and must be carried back down the treacherous creek bed route. Carrying two kids is not difficult. Carrying two kids, two purses, a very expensive camera, and oh, a huge-ass tree, is decidedly more difficult.

I grab the boy and the bags, Becky grabs the crying girl and the huge tree. Becky wants to get down the creek bed as quickly as possible, so she is doing a brisk walk ahead of me. Vivian starts to slide down away from her grasp, so with the tree under one arm and Vivian flailing under the other arm Becky picks up her pace. She is just trying to get to the end of this adventure as quickly as she can, but the visual I have in front of me looks like a scene out of a movie titled *Not Without My Daughter and My Tree.*

We finally get back down to the pickup point. We are all dirty, bloody, and tear-stained.

I snap a photo.

Our Christmas cards are going to look like Save the Children ads this year.

Fa la la friggin' la.

YOU MAY CONSIDER VIOLENCE

14

Kids bring out the best in all of us

BAD NEWS: It's illegal to lock your kid in a closet.
GOOD NEWS: You *can* lock yourself in a closet.

$\mathcal{H}$ ERE'S THE THING. Most of us are relatively sane people. We brought children into this world with the intention to love and protect them. Perhaps we thought we would even teach them a thing or two along the way. It was all going to be so beautiful.

Except now your little ball of boy beauty is pulling the cat's tail and you're left with an overwhelming urge to spank his bottom as a consequence for hurting an animal. You are, of course, a horrible, horrible person and parent for even letting such thoughts cross your mind. And you aren't quite sure when the beauty is supposed to kick in.

I was spanked once when I was a kid, when I was about two years old. My dad saw the little red mark it left on my little baby butt and he never spanked me again. Even in my teenage years, when I really, really deserved it. But when Vivian first entered her toddler years I was frequently overwhelmed with the desire to spank her. Maybe she would hit one of the dogs, hard. Maybe she would hit me, hard. Maybe she would go limp when I went to pick her up, and then she would also start kicking, flailing her arms, and screaming at the same time. Maybe she did this out in public somewhere.

I'm a pretty calm person; it takes a lot to get me riled up. These types of Vivian antics really riled me. I would feel my temper start to flare, and in those moments my instinct was to smack her bottom. Sometimes I would actually spank her. I guess it was an attempt to snap her out of her bad behavior, to let her know what was not acceptable. The spank was never very hard, and the fact that she had a diaper on meant she barely felt the smack. But anytime I actually smacked her bottom she would look at me and cry, then I would start crying too. Because I was a horrible parent who was one step away from beating her child with a belt.

I think that is why it is difficult to have an honest discussion about spanking, because when you think about striking a child your mind instantly flashes to a kid hovering in the corner, covered in bruises and welts, while a raging parent beats the crap out of the tender young thing. As a parent, if you spank your child—no matter how light the smack, or how heavily padded the butt—you instantly fear you are that raging parent. And you are instantly covered in shame. You don't talk to anyone about how your kid is pushing you to your limit, because then others would imagine you beating the crap out of your kid, and then you would have even more shame. So instead of getting help you just get quiet and are left to navigate this scary issue all by your-self, all while assuming that you are the only parent who is this horrible.

I never felt comfortable with spanking Vivian, mostly because the spanking didn't really represent discipline: what the spanking really represented was my losing control—of the situation and of myself. After doing it a few times Becky and I decided we weren't going to spank anymore, because both of us hated ourselves for doing it. We would, however, still say, "Do you want a spank-ing?" as a way to let Vivian know we were serious. But I started to feel uncomfortable with that as well. I didn't like even threat-ening to hit the child; it felt like the wrong way to get her to do what we wanted.

Also, Vivian is a very sensitive kid: putting her in a time-out, or speaking forcefully, seems to actually be as or more effective than spanking ever was. That's probably because getting put in a time-out doesn't end up with Mommy on the floor crying. The lesson can be a bit confusing when Mommy is mad at you one second, giving you a spanking the next second, and then profusely apologizing while hugging you the second after that. "Get a hold of your mood swings, lady."

Child psychologist Katie Hurley acknowledges that parenting can push you to a breaking point, but reminds parents that spanking is not an advisable form of discipline. "Although kids might push parents to a point of wanting to push back in a similar manner, spanking can have significant long-term consequences for children. It can lead to anxiety, depression, and even substance abuse in later years. It also teaches children to solve problems with aggression."

My spanking instinct usually kicks in when the kids are hurting another person or animal. The biggest hiccup I always have about spanking the kids in these situations is that smacking a kid while saying "No hitting!" is faulty reasoning at best. At worst it's just giving them more ideas about ways to hit others. Neither of these sounds productive to the long-term goal: that my children not do things that make me want to smack them.

Child psychologist Gail Marie Poverman-Kave confirms my misgivings about the effectiveness of spanking as a disciplinary tool. "Hitting someone teaches one thing and one thing only: that when you deem yourself angry enough, you are allowed to hit another person or living thing. In the real world, we would never put up with that. We don't want to model behaviors for our children that we don't want to see in them. We can *want* to hit them—as long as we don't. Trust me. I'm Italian. There have been plenty of times that I've *wanted* to hit my two—I just never have."

With this, Gail touches on why I wanted to write about this topic. I don't think it's acknowledged enough that as parents we are often pushed to the point of wanting to spank our kids. It's not just a joke to say, "My kids are driving me crazy!" Sometimes it feels as if they are literally driving you crazy. So crazy that you actually felt the urge to smack a child. This wasn't part of your dream of becoming a mom.

Some kids seem to make it their life's goal to push their parents to their crazy point. Then, once they see they officially have control over your brain matter, they keep pushing. One of my MOFL told me she's had spanking urges with only one of her two kids. One of her kids is what could be described as "spirited" and at times possibly "challenging." I'd probably also add "too smart for his own good." This child knows when he's pushed a situation to the limit, then enjoys seeing what lies on the other side of that line. But that child's sibling is much calmer. The sibling pushes as well, but when he sees he's starting to rile up Mommy or Daddy, instead of actively trying to make things worse, he maneuvers out of the situation, deploying his adorableness to defuse the tension.

My peak spanking inclination occurred for both kids right around the beginning of their toddler years, when they were are at their peak rebellion stage. A time when "No" became their default response because "Yes" would have been too easy. And toddlers are never interested in the easy route. The transition from adorable baby to stubborn hellion took me by surprise both times. And both times I was at a loss for how to control these children.

I didn't quite know what to do with my monkeys, who wanted to experiment with exactly how far they could push their independence and my sanity. Once I had a little experience dealing with the hellions, my arsenal no longer needed to include spanking, because in our case, it was more of a kneejerk reaction to an unexpected bump in the road.

Vivian's behavior has gotten better as she's grown older, but I really think her improving communication skills are the reason I stopped having spanking urges. If I get upset with her these days, I can get down to eye level and clearly communicate what actions I did not appreciate. If I put her on a time-out she understands why and is appropriately traumatized by her punishment. So much so that even mentioning a time-out is usually enough to fix her behavior, because she remembers that she didn't like her last time-out.

Daniel, on the other hand, is still toddling around in his monkey phase. I try to reason with him or explain why his behavior is bad, but he only focuses on how to maneuver out of my grip. And it's as if his memory of whatever event I'm trying to discuss with him fades out of his mind before the event is even over. I feel like I can spend entire days putting Daniel on one time-out after another for the exact same behavior, which he does over and over again. When I put him on the time-out stair and hold him there he just giggles. He hasn't yet learned that laughing in the face of an upset parent is just about the absolute worst thing kids can do if they are in any way interested in remaining on this Earth.

Child psychologist Katie Hurley gives this advice for dealing with challenging moments before they happen: "I often encourage parents to keep a journal of the high-intensity triggers in their homes. What are the behaviors that cause the most significant emotional reactions for the parents? Is it talking back? Is it hitting? What is happening when these behaviors most often occur?

Close to dinnertime? Sleepless night the night before? When parents journal their own triggers, responses, and potential causes of the behaviors at play, they can learn to troubleshoot in advance."

Katie is correct that the best way to deal with the insanity your child brings on is to have a plan in place before the insanity arrives. So, after we decided spanking was off the table as a discipline option, we had to come up with other ways to deal with the insanity.

Like any other challenges I've faced during this parenting attempt, this one has gotten easier over time. I'm better at controlling my initial burst of anger. As my first reaction, I now just remove the child from the situation, to give myself time to calm down. Sometimes Becky or I will hand the other a child and walk away, which is our universal "I can't deal with this kid" signal. And if one of us senses the other is getting riled up, we'll intervene as the voice of reason to calm the situation.

If you're dealing with this spanking issue, your first step is to get past the shame associated with it. Understand that you are not the first parent in the history of time to deal with being pushed to your limit. Acknowledge that it is happening, talk to your partner about it, and come up with tools to help calm yourself *before* you're actually in the middle of a stressful situation.

Also, I think it's really important to have time away from your kids—time to decompress, relax, and regroup. I think we're equipped to deal with only so much crap before we snap, and sometimes we need to go shake off the crap so we can come back and not explode when presented with whatever wonders our children have prepared for us.

- -

This can mean taking a night out with your friends, a trip alone to the store, or even a twenty-minute bubble bath (see Chapter 9: You May Start Playing Bunco). Sometimes parents need to replenish their reserves, just as athletes need to stay hydrated, because Lord knows, parenting is a physical and mental challenge.

Moms on the Front Lines

SPANKING?

I asked my MOFL for their thoughts on spanking and any tips they have for avoiding it.

One admitted, "Don't judge me, but yes!! I have spanked. I was over-the-top upset and I couldn't help myself. It was only a couple times. I had no idea what kind of parent I was going to be but I'm guilty of having said, 'I would never do that when I'm a mom.' Well, shit. Turns out I did."

Brooke has advice for the times when your lovely child is pulling the poor cat's tail. "It's so hard because they hit the animal and then you do want to spank them and say 'No hitting,' which doesn't make a lot of sense when you think about it. In our house we first stop the behavior by physically holding the child's hands down, then we demonstrate 'nice pats,' and then when they keep doing it, because they always do, we remove the child for time-out. Then, when they come back and do it again, you just lock the kid outside. (Just kidding!)"

Yes, Brooke is just kidding about locking her kid outside, but she is touching on the most frustrating part of dealing with disobedient children: there is no one way to deal with them. And even if you find a way that works today, it probably won't work tomorrow. And meanwhile your poor cat has developed a nervous twitch thanks to your toddler. It's all crazy-making.

Michelle, mom of two, has a strategy to calm herself. "If I feel I'm about to 'lose it' I count to ten. After counting I'm usually calm enough to deal with the situation without spanking. If I am still just as angry I put the child in a time-out so that I can calm down. It's more like a mommy time-out."

I like the idea of a mommy time-out and think I may start putting myself on some. Why do the kids get to be the ones to sit alone in their awesome rooms when they've driven their parents insane? I say leave the kids to their insanity and go take a long nice bubble bath instead of engaging with them. No spanking, no crying—*and* bubbles! This is one of my better ideas.

Sarah G. does not have a no-spanking rule in her house. "We've spanked and feel comfortable with spanking as a tool for child-rearing when appropriate. It's something that has occurred only a handful of times because there are instances of safety where you need to quickly make a big impression on a small child. A child psychologist taught at our moms' group and said within certain age groups and certain behaviors, it can communicate volumes. I think if spanking is a tool and you can use it judiciously and when you're in control, it can be good."

One of my MOFL said she tried spanking but knew it wasn't right for her son. "He started spanking me back when he didn't like something I was doing. I think every child is different, but Love and Logic's time-out method seemed to work a lot better for my son."

I attended a few Love and Logic classes because so many of my MOFL recommended them for learning how to deal with my kids calmly. The basic premise of Love and Logic is to come at your kids with empathy instead of aggression. For instance, "Ahhh, that is so sad that your toy broke when you threw it across the room, that's such a bummer." You would use that instead of "Stop throwing your toys! You just broke one! Come here so I can spank you!" You can see a subtle difference.

The idea behind Love and Logic is that by staying calm, you are helping your children to connect their actions with their consequences. If you get angry and yell, then their attention shifts to being mad at you for disciplining them—instead of being mad at themselves for breaking their toys. The goal is to raise kids who eventually will make the decision to not throw the toy— even when you aren't around.

Love and Logic also recommends simply saying, "Uh-oh!" every time your kid does something that would be time-out-worthy. All you say is, "Uh-oh!" in a regular calm voice, then remove the child from the situation for time-out wherever it's convenient: a corner, a stair, a room. After trying this a few times with Vivian, now the mere uttering of "Uh-oh!" terrifies her more than any spanking threat ever did. Daniel, on the other hand, just starts repeating "Uh-oh!" back to me in the same singsongy voice I've used. Logic isn't his strong suit, it would seem.

REMEMBER WHEN VACATIONS WERE FUN?

15

Hotel rooms are modern torture chambers

THANK GOD IT'S MONDAY

"Why are you so happy? It's your first Monday back to work after your weeklong vacation with your family."

"Because it's my first day away from my family in a week."

$\mathcal{T}$HE YEAR BEFORE I had my first kid a friend of mine asked if I'd be interested in going to Cuba. Yes! I even made the suggestion that we ("we" being four women with maybe four words of Spanish amongst us) rent a car and drive across Cuba, to get a real feel for the land. Smash cut to the four of us lost in the middle of Cuba, in the middle of the night, in the middle of a torrential downpour.

All this is to say: I'm up for adventure.

Right before we boarded our plane home, I was pulled out of line. A man I did not understand took me to an underground room for reasons I did not understand. A woman was passed out in the corner of the room.

I'm still not quite sure what the hell was going on or why I was taken there (I think it was something to do with my luggage being full of rum), but the thought of returning to that room does not seem even remotely as scary as taking two kids to a hotel. Indeed, even I, former world traveler and an "up for anything" girl, shudder at the thought of traveling with my two kids.

Hotels used to signify a place to relax, kick up my feet, let someone else do the cooking—maybe even put my meal on a table pulled right up to the bed for maximum gluttony. But, with the addition of children, hotel rooms become torture chambers. There is no relaxing with toddlers in a hotel room. (Granted, there is no relaxing with toddlers anywhere.) In this hotel, the only feet being kicked up are the children's, which are kicking at each other out of boredom with the offerings of this small chamber. With small kids, even room service sucks. Yes, someone else cooks the food, but that just increases the chances that said food will not meet the unapologetically discriminating palate of our young diners. "Mommy, these chicken nuggets don't taste good, they are too long."

We've gone for a quick night away with both kids a couple of times, but nothing that would qualify as an official vacation. I'm still not quite sure how taking our whole family and plopping them in a different location is a vacation from anything, exactly. Are we vacationing from our routine? From everything that makes my kids feel comfortable and secure? From separate bedrooms? Boy, does that sound rejuvenating.

Whenever the topic of a family vacation comes up I always say, "Maybe in like a year." I've been saying that for four years now. Maybe once the kids are in their twenties we'll finally be ready to take the leap.

Moms on the Front Lines

"VACATIONING"

I asked my MOFL about their experiences with family vacations. Their responses are not getting me any closer to booking that Disneyland trip.

Dana, mom of two, failed to sell me on the idea. "I don't mind flying with my kids unless it's to and from Hawaii with a ten-month-old baby on antibiotics (think fifteen dirty diapers) for an ear infection (think ear infection and pressure). On the flight home from Hawaii I think my husband and I both considered jumping out the emergency exit door—while we were in the air. It was awful. I also hate hotel rooms with little kids. I will spring for a condo or something with a separate bedroom for the kids any day. If we do stay in a hotel, I have come to the realization that they will not nap *at all* and we will *all* be up at 5:00 AM."

You had me at "condo or something with a separate bedroom," then lost me again with "up at 5:00 AM."

Jill has a pretty solid strategy if you're still using a Pack 'n Play. "We used to make sure that we had a separate room for the kids. Then, when one wouldn't go to sleep, we would move her in her Pack 'n Play into the bathroom. (Sounds weird, I know.) She needed to be alone and she would go right to sleep."

Next time, *I* may just sleep in the bathroom. It sounds peaceful.

Deanna paints a picture of a thrilling time. "Vacationing has always been a challenge for us so we don't do it often. I remember when we had to stay at a hotel with Kate when she was about fifteen months. We were very naive in thinking we were just going to put her in the Pack 'n Play and then she would go to sleep while we were still in the room. After about an hour of sitting in the dark and listening to her singing, talking, and playing, we ended up driving around with her until she fell asleep."

Kaysee's three children are clearly better behaved than mine. "Start young and it will be totally normal to the kids! Our kids love airports, airplanes, and hotels. As long as you are prepared with snacks and a small backpack of toys, the kids should do great during travel. I myself enjoy hotels because we all get to spend time together without so many distractions of work or laundry or daily life. As long as there is a beach or amusement for the kids, vacationing is fun!"

I'm pretty sure I might just pay Kaysee to take my kids vacationing for me; she sounds up for the task.

Or, better yet, I'll take Michelle's advice: "Leave them with Grandma while you vacation without them!"

Sold.

Journal Entry

A RELAXING TIME BY THE SEA

We make our one and only attempt at a family vacation when I am five months pregnant with Daniel. Vivian has just turned two years old, and we are all getting over a cold. There is no way we can possibly see this going wrong.

The three-hour drive to the ocean with an unhappily restrained toddler has been quite an undertaking. Once we get to the hotel, things just continue their slide downhill. We have a small hotel room near the beach. It has a little balcony and fresh air sweeping through it. Vivian is bored within five minutes.

We dumped the contents of her playroom into the car before we left, hoping to keep her entertained. It is an unsuccessful attempt. She is used to having a big house to run around in. Hanging out in one small room is confusing to her. Especially

>

because all the adults want to do is lie on the bed and relax for a minute. She isn't having any of that. The only way there might be any of that is if the TV in the room has a DVD player. Pixar would save the day for us, but with no DVD player we are doomed. We try to show Vivian movies on her iPad, but she keeps getting upset that she can't watch them on the actual TV right in front of her. We'd have better luck convincing her that gravity doesn't exist.

We decide to get her out of the room and go to the hotel restaurant for dinner. She is usually really good in restaurants. That night she decides to shake things up a bit. The restaurant is a fancy one, the kind where you feel weird even speaking in your normal voice because it's so damn quiet. It is the kind of place where silverware clanging the plates makes up most of the noise. That is, until Vivian makes her appearance.

She instantly transforms into a two-year-old right at the table. She is whining and crying and talking and banging her silverware on the table. We negotiate, threaten, plead for mercy. Nothing works. We last about ten minutes before I demand that Becky take the hellion back to the hotel room while I wait for our dinner.

When I get back to the room, Vivian is all smiles, unaffected by her exile. We crowd around one small end table and eat our $100 meal. It is so relaxing.

We all go to bed when Vivi goes to bed, and we all wake up fifteen times throughout the night when she wakes up scared. After about the twelfth wake-up, we take her out of the Pack 'n Play and put her in bed with us. She instantly falls soundly asleep. With her head against one of our throats, and her feet against the other's kidneys. We are each left with approximately four inches of bed on which to get a comfortable four hours of sleep before Vivian decides it is time to embrace the day.

The day itself goes pretty well, with walks to the beach and a relatively uneventful dining experience at lunch. Unfortunately, because Vivi is just getting over a cold, she doesn't have a lot of reserves. And because she is in a weird place the chances of getting her to nap are nil. This exhaustion rears its head around 6:00 PM. It takes the form of an epic meltdown.

After two hours of trying to distract her with games and stickers and pay-per-view children's programming, I officially call it. While Becky bounces the crying Vivian around the room, just as she used to do when she was a baby, I pack and load. I am done with this trip and cannot bear the thought of another horrible night's sleep. Once the car is packed we snap the screaming child into her car seat and take off for our three-hour drive home. It is dark, I am tired, and Becky has promised to stay awake to keep me entertained with conversation. She and Vivian both pass out within fifteen minutes.

That three-hour drive home is the most peaceful part of our trip.

16 LET'S LEAN BACK, NOT IN

Who has the energy for ambition?

RISE AND SHINE

"I'm 'Leaning In' to my pillow."

"You might have misunderstood the point of the Lean In movement."

"I don't have the energy for movement."

A FEW YEARS AGO a book came out titled *Lean In: Women, Work, and the Will to Lead.* Written by Sheryl Sandberg, the COO of Facebook, it's all about empowering women, especially women in the workplace. The Lean In movement focuses on "encouraging women to pursue their ambitions, and changing the conversation from what we can't do to what we can do." In short, "You are women. Go roar and stuff."

The idea is that we need to change the workplace landscape so that ambitious women are perceived in a positive light. There are ways to not give up on that career ambition once children come into the picture. There is enough room in women's lives for both a successful family and a successful career. Roar.

This all sounds fantastic in theory, because *yay, women!* But in actual execution I'm not sure I have the energy for this movement. I don't know that it is possible to really lean in to both career and kids. Yes, you can make room for both, but can you really kick the amount of ass that *Lean In* is saying you can? Is there enough coffee in the world for such things?

Before I had kids I was crazy ambitious, and went about my career a little differently than most. I was working in a cubicle, doing accounting, when I decided I needed to do something creative with my life. So I took a few classes, learned a few creative computer programs, then worked nights and weekends building a portfolio of work. I was given an opportunity by a small business that needed both a designer and a bookkeeper. *Bam,* I had my in. I worked my butt off at that job, took my work home to make it even better, and worked unpaid overtime to help the company. I also slowly built a freelance business of side clients on word of mouth and networking. I worked nights and weekends to build up my freelance business. Eventually, after years and years, I went out on my own and started working completely for myself.

By the time I started having kids, my business and clientele were secure enough that I could simply keep up with current clients and not focus at all on growing. This was imperative, because I honestly don't see how I could have been present for my baby while still in a business-building mode. There were just not enough hours in the day, and I just wasn't sleeping enough of those hours to be in any shape for ambition.

These days I work an average of three days a week, sometimes more, sometimes less. I am in a unique profession where I can set my own hours and still keep up with the demands of my job. If things are busy, I can work after I put the kids to bed, sacrificing sleep for the sake of keeping all the balls in the air. I am a working/stay-at-home hybrid in that I can usually make time for daytime kid classes or school events, but I also pull in a paycheck.

But at the same time I don't think I'm very good at either side of my hybrid. My stay-at-home mom friends seem to always have their shit together so much better than I do, and I know for a fact I've left career opportunities on the table over the last four years because I just didn't have the time or energy to shift into work overdrive. If I were to "lean in" and fully kick ass at *either* working or staying at home, it would be nearly impossible to keep the other duty even functioning, let alone thriving.

That's where I think *Lean In* fails. It fails to acknowledge that you can't really lean in to work without leaning out from your kids, especially in your kids' early years. The kind of women that *Lean In* speaks to are the kind of women who like to be good at stuff. They are ambitious and competitive. Those women will want to be just as good at parenting as they are at their jobs, and they will be keenly aware that they are missing out on time with their kids while they kick ass at work.

But all of this leads me to one of the main issues behind this entire discussion. The Lean In movement seems to me to be a decidedly elitist concept. It imagines a world where women are able to choose between working and staying home with their kids. Most of the time that choice is a financial one and not a matter of ambition. Many working women would probably love to stay home with their kids (or at least think they would, grass being greener and all that), but it's not possible to raise their family on just one income.

I guess *Lean In* would encourage women in the workplace, no matter their reason for being there, to not let anything hold them back from trying to achieve more professionally. But I think it misses the mark on that point too. There is something to be said for not constantly striving for more, for just doing your job and doing it well and not worrying about where your next promotion lies.

There is always a lot of discussion about why women aren't in more positions of power. Why we aren't better represented in government or as CEOs of companies. The thought is, if we had more of our sisters calling the shots, the rules might begin to bend more in our favor. Issues that are important to our day-to-day lives would be important to those in power. And then we would start to see positive change in policies that affect women.

Many think that it is a lack of equality that keeps women from achieving positions of power—that the fabled glass ceiling still exists. One of the biggest complaints of the Lean In community is that women in power (or any job, really) are held to a different standard when it comes to characteristics and behavior. For instance, when a woman is assertive she is a bitch, whereas when a man is assertive he's seen as having leadership potential. Also, women can be held back professionally because they need things like maternity leave and flexible work schedules once they have kids. The thought is that men are able to rise up the ladder to success because they are expected to rise, which leaves women constantly fighting against the fact that we're still not really welcome on the ladder at all.

While I agree that there is still sexism in the world, and in the business world specifically, I think there is more working against us than just outside forces. I think a lot of the time, women take themselves off the ladder; they aren't pushed. And that is one of the main focuses of *Lean In,* to encourage women to lean in to success and ambition instead of excluding themselves.

But what if they don't want to lean in? What if a majority of women don't have the drive to be the leader of a political party or the CEO of a huge corporation? What if most women have a different gauge for what success means to them? And their version of success doesn't involve working fifteen-hour days, networking after work hours, and engaging in the level of bullshit required to navigate to the top?

I really, really enjoy working. I have since I was a teenager. Putting in the hard work it took to build my business, chase my dreams, and find an uncommon level of professional success has been tremendously rewarding to me. But I know plenty of women who could give two poops about building a career. It's just not how they are wired. Maybe they are invigorated by being present for their kids' childhoods, or maybe they work but only because it means they can use their paychecks to provide a nice house and occasional vacation for their family.

So maybe I do agree with *Lean In*. I do agree that we are women, and we should roar. But maybe we need to acknowledge that we roar in different ways, some louder than others, but all equally as valid. And also, we need to acknowledge that it is very difficult to roar from beneath a pile of poopy diapers.

Moms on the Front Lines
FAMILY AND CAREER

As I mentioned, I used to work a lot. The past five years spent making and raising babies have left me operating at about 70 percent of my professional capabilities—probably even less than that during each child's first six months or so. With Daniel getting older I'm just now starting to feel like I might be able to get back up to speed a little, and it's exciting. But at the same time, I want to balance time with the kids while they are young: there will always be opportunities to work hard, but the kids will be little for only a few years. So I reached out to my MOFL to ask if their careers have taken a hit since having kids, and how they try to balance family and work.

Like me, **Sarah B.**, who is a veterinarian, had worked very hard to establish her career before she had kids. "I don't feel like having kids hindered my professional career at all. But I have a good schedule. I work four ten-hour days a week, so I get three full days with the boys."

Sarah also mentioned that she has a very supportive boss who understands the demands of family, which makes it much easier for her to balance family and work life. She acknowledges that not everyone is so lucky in that regard.

Michelle, mom of two boys, is looking to mix work with staying home. "Having kids is definitely limiting my options. I want to do something part-time, but everything I'm looking at is full-time. It's frustrating."

After initially staying home a few years with her kids, **Sarah G.** went back to work because her family needed the second income. "No, I don't think having kids has hurt my career trajectory. But, having kids has changed how I prioritize my time. So, focusing on 'moving up the ladder' just isn't important to me. I don't want a demanding job; I relish my flexibility!"

I asked Sarah G. if she thought it was practical to think that women can be super competitive at work while still being good moms. She thinks that most women don't have that mindset. "I don't even think it's about what's practical, but what your heart desires. I think most women seek out options that allow them to be available to their family because they *want* to be available. I don't think having children limits you at all—it just changes what's important to you."

Kaysee, mom of three, had her priorities change as her family grew. "I definitely think that becoming a parent changes everything! I worked a lot before having children. With the first I still worked a fair amount, then when the second came I had a nanny. Now with three I am a parent first and work when I can. Luckily I'm in a flexible business where I can do a lot from home. Priorities definitely have changed! I give props to any parent who works a full-time job and has children."

Tara, mom of one, picked her career because of its flexibility. "I chose a career path, teaching, that is very conducive to raising a family, so it has not hindered my career. I have been able to job share and work part-time with minimal sacrifices. This is allowing me to be the mom I want to be and maintain a career. I'm hoping that working part-time keeps my experience relevant enough to take my career in the direction I hope to go."

I asked Tara if she feels that taking a step back from teaching full-time will hurt her down the road, if she thinks that it will be difficult to regain her footing professionally once she's ready again. "In my line of work," she told me, "I don't think it will be difficult to regain my footing. Yes, if I was to stop working altogether, but that is why I have chosen to continue to work part-time. Without a doubt my family is my priority, so I don't lose sleep at night over a missed career opportunity. I have goals and ambitions (and expenses), but I am not a career-driven person; I am a family person. If I am leaning in to anything, it is myself. I love my time with Drew and I love my job. It is a great balance."

Brooke, mom of two, worked part-time after her first baby and has become a full-time stay-at-home mom now that she has two. Seeing Brooke in action always makes me feel so insecure about my overall parenting skills. She crafts, hosts elaborately themed play dates, and has a level of calm with her children that makes me think she might be heavily medicated. Not that there's anything wrong with that.

Brooke told me about her gradual journey to stay-at-home mom. "We always planned for me to be home with kids. After my first baby, I think I felt like I could manage more and work a flexible schedule without missing too much. I worked until I had baby #2. We did not want daycare and felt like the privilege of being able to stay at home was our priority. It was difficult to not go back to work, since I worked in a career that I not only loved but was also incredibly flexible after I had one little one, so I would have enjoyed being able to continue working after two kids. I do miss working on those days when the kids cry all day and move from one fight to another. But I truly enjoy being at home and feel very lucky to not have to have my children in daycare."

If you want a glimpse at the joy that is staying home with your kids, note Brooke's postscript: "I just typed this as Blake pushed the recliner button making me recline then sit back up *over* and *over*. Then he peed on the floor in 'Princess Sydney's Room' as she yelled, 'You don't pee in a princess's room!'"

I reached out to one of my friends, **Rachel**, who spent over ten years building her high-powered career before she had kids. She is one of the most ambitious women I know, so I was interested to find out how she approaches her work/life balance.

I was surprised to learn that Rachel wants to stay home with her kids full-time. "I cannot do the job I used to do and be the type of mom I want to be. *Lean In* pretends that it's possible to do both. I don't want to lean in. I want to be a good mom. *Lean In* assumes that a woman thinks it is more important to climb the ladder than to be home. The whole problem is the perception that being home with your kids is less important than being a CEO. My dad and my husband literally cannot wrap their heads around me wanting to be home. They can't picture me doing it, because I was an ass-kicker at work. But now I want to kick ass at home."

This is very interesting to me: the ambitious women are still focused on being the best at whatever they are doing—they've just changed what they're focused on.

Karen, who is raising her daughter alone, has found leaning in to be tremendously positive for both herself and her daughter. "As a single mom I have a different perspective. Having a daughter drove me to make a change, for the better, to a different company that gave me the flexibility and freedom to put my daughter first when necessary. As the *Lean In* book says, a woman *can* do it all (with or without a 50:50 partner). I have specific rules that I stick to at least 90 percent of the time: my laptop and phone are off for work-related issues when my daughter is awake. After she goes to sleep it's an entirely different thing. When I travel for work I work my butt off, but when I am home, I leave work at 4:30 PM to pick her up every day. Does it suck to miss all the after-hours work functions? Yes, sometimes. But your priorities change with children. I am blessed to be able to be a great example to my daughter of a successful and smart career woman who can also be a mom. So in a nutshell, I don't think my career would have taken off like it has if not for becoming a mom. It pushed me out of my comfort zone so that I could make the best life for my daughter. She made me lean in more instead of less."

How much do I love how different all these women are? In this small sampling of moms we have such a diversity of thoughts, approaches, and lifestyles. I have a lot of respect for each one of these moms and the jobs they're doing with their kids. *Lean In*, to me, seems like a rather simple concept that is difficult to apply to the complex realities of modern-day families and women. But the general idea is one I can get behind: empowering women to empower themselves, in whatever form that might take. We are empowering for our generation, and for our daughters'.

I think all my MOFL are doing a great job roaring their asses off. Cheers, ladies.

YOU WILL NEVER HAVE ANOTHER CONVERSATION

Teaching them to talk was not your best idea

HEALTHY COMMUNICATION

*I*T CAN BE an exciting time when your little baby monkey starts becoming an actual human being, and one of the milestones of that transition is when your kid starts talking. Finally there are real words coming out of their mouths, instead of just grunts, babbles, and fart noises (I feel like babies are born with the innate ability to make and be entertained by mouth-produced fart noises).

Currently Daniel, at eighteen months, says, "Ho, ho, ho!" every time he sees a picture of Santa. This, of course, makes us all declare him a genius. Having spent the last year and a half trying to decipher his whines and finger-pointing, hearing him start putting actual real words to real things is the beginning of something great. Would it have been a *little* more convenient if he'd started to put words to something other than a mythical figure we only talk about once a year? Perhaps. But I'll take my "ho, ho, ho"s where I can get them.

I remember there being a distinct improvement in all of our lives when Vivian could actually start communicating her thoughts. No longer did she have to scream at the top of her lungs because we were unable to read her mind. I could see that so much of her traditionally "toddler-like" behavior had stemmed from her general frustration with the world—frustration that her body couldn't keep up with her mind. She wanted to go everywhere and tell us all sorts of things, but her physical and speech abilities weren't quite there yet. However, her screaming abilities were well honed, so she just relied heavily on those. It was a special time.

Once she started talking, I could see her start to breathe a little easier and unclench a bit. Life was no longer one big struggle to get her point across. Granted, she only knew a few words, but even being able to say yes and no to questions was a game-changer.

That's not to say there weren't hiccups along the way. Especially when, even though the child was speaking, no one had any idea what the hell she was saying. Vivian was always so patient with us as we asked her over and over again to repeat what she had said. Each time she would repeat her words exactly the same, and each time we'd give her the exact same baffled look. "Show me" and "Can you point to it?" became common responses to our language barrier. It was sorta like charades with the person acting out the phrase just repeating it over and over again. In Japanese.

One time Vivian had a huge meltdown for twenty minutes after I gave her spaghetti for lunch. She kept asking, through screeching tears, for the "big sauce." I got the jar of spaghetti sauce out, thinking she wanted to see it for some reason. The screaming continued, as did the demand. After I don't know how long, I just started bringing things one at a time from the fridge, trying anything to stop this episode. She finally stopped crying when I brought out the container of salsa. She pointed at it: "Big sauce!" Dear Lord.

One of the biggest goals in our house when our kids learn to speak is to teach them proper manners (despite, ahem, my story above of allowing my child to scream endlessly until she got what she wanted). They have limited vocabulary, so it's easy for them to just spew off one-word demands. These get their point across, we hop into action, and all is well with the world. Except for the fact that we're then raising a-holes (who demand a great variety of sauces).

One of Daniel's first words was "please." He has no idea what it means, but he knows that he needs to say it to get anything he wants. Now when he wants something he will just point at it and say, "Pwease" over and over again. This is probably not exactly what we are going for in building a polite young man, but it's a start.

One time when Vivian was just under two years old we took her to get her hair cut. As we waited for our appointment we watched another little boy getting his hair cut. He had been given a few M&M's to bribe him into sitting still during his haircut. When he finished his last M&M he said to his grandma, "More M&M's!" His grandma looked at him, shook her head, and said, "How do you ask?" To which he promptly replied, "May I have some more M&M's please, Grandma?"

Becky and I looked at each other and instantly felt inferior. (Note that this is a regular feeling.) We were lucky to get a one-word demand out of Vivi, while this kid was speaking in complete, respectful sentences. When we asked his grandma how old the boy was, we learned he was almost three. We were a little relieved, but we still knew we had only a year to teach our kid how to be a proper human when it came to talking.

Thereafter, that little boy set the standard whenever Vivian asked for something. We'd say, "How do you ask?" She would answer with, *blank stare*. Then we would prompt, "May I . . ." She would repeat, "May I . . ." We would say, "Keep going." So she would keep going: "May I, may I, may I?" It was a long road, to say the least.

As fun as it is to hear words finally make their way out of your child's mouth and start to form real live sentences, things have a way of taking a turn relatively soon after this new skill introduces itself. For instance, your initial excitement becomes quickly tempered when you realize that this child is never, ever going to shut the hell up ever again. And, oh my goodness, what you wouldn't give for a few grunts and whines instead of your now-constant background music: "Mama, Mama, Mama, guess what?" "What" ends up being a forty-five-minute monologue on spiders, the cat, JELL-O, and Bubble Guppies. You are essentially now living with a crackhead with ADD. Warn your poor ears.

Ever since Vivian found her voice, Becky and I have found it nearly impossible to finish any conversation. Between our crap memories and the fact that we never actually complete a thought when we're together, we haven't effectively communicated any pertinent information to each other in two years.

"I told you about that the other night at dinner."

"No, you *started* to tell me about that at dinner, but then Vivian had to tell us all about her mosquito bite."

"Why didn't I finish the story later?"

"Because we were too busy not finishing ten other stories we started. Just text me next time."

My MOFL also struggle with children who never stop talking. Jen has found it twice as difficult to have a real conversation now that both her kids are talking. "Seriously impossible!!" she pointed out. "Especially when there is more than one child. Competition!!"

Michelle has tried to come up with an alternate time to communicate full thoughts. "Date nights are usually the only time we get to have actual conversations. We try to have them at least once a month so we can connect."

Sarah B. has just given up. "We can't talk about anything important until they go to bed. By then we're so tired that we usually forget."

With three kids in the house, Deanna and her husband constantly lose their battle to converse. "I swear, the kids will be playing in the other room, and as soon as they hear us begin to talk they come running into the room with something they need to say! We actually started having 'date night' once a week just to be able to talk. We put the kids to bed and eat dinner together after they're in bed."

I love this don't-actually-leave-the-house date night. Anything you can do in sweats always sounds like a good plan to me.

For your own sanity I highly recommend avoiding any attempts at real conversation when your children are still new to talking. You will only succeed at giving yourself a twitch from constantly being interrupted mid-thought. That can't be good for your already maxed-out brain. In our house we constantly tell Vivian it's rude to interrupt, and try to teach her to say, "Excuse me," before interjecting. But her brain is too busy coming up with the next thing to say to worry about such formalities.

Most of our dinnertime conversation happens right after dinner, when the kids have been excused and we're cleaning up the plates. The children are distracted by playing, and we look preoccupied with cleaning so they don't bother us, for fear they may be asked to help with said cleaning. That seven minutes is our only time in the evening to communicate any important facts of the day. It's a session of speed communicating that usually ends with, "Just email me anything really important I should know."

I will say that, besides the fact that they'll take over every conversation from now until they start giving you the silent treatment in their preteen years, having a talking kid is overall a pretty great step in the right direction. I mean, you've been talking to a monkey for the past two years and all of a sudden it has started talking back. If nothing else, having kids that can keep up their end of a conversation tends to make the whole communication thing much more enjoyable. At least it makes it easier, because your little former monkies usually end up not only keeping up their end of the conversation, but also completely taking over your end as well. Which means you can sit back and relax while their young, nimble brains do all the work.

Pretty much every day my four-year-old says something that cracks me up. Sometimes it's the actual words coming out of her mouth, or maybe it's her inflection or accompanying facial expression. She is still young enough that I am constantly amazed that this little person I made *inside* my body is now telling me elaborate stories and delivering awesome punch lines. I love to sit back and listen to her talk, to see the intricacies of her brain coming out in real time as she tirelessly reports every thought that comes into her head.

When we're over at my mom's house, one of my favorite things in the world is to listen to the two of them, my mother and my daughter, sitting by themselves in another room, carrying on an elaborate conversation. It tickles me to watch their relationship grow and to think of my mom patiently listening to my endless chattering when I was Vivian's age. Come to think of it, the way she talks to Vivian isn't much different from how she still talks to me. There is a *small* possibility I've yet to grow out of my rambling phase.

CHRISTMAS EVE ATTIRE

Toy you will spend 13 hours assembling

(child will play with this box instead)

EASY ASSEMBLY ONLY 3,875 PIECES!

fun fun fun

only 762 pieces!

INSTRUCTIONS

ABIES "R" US SHOULD sell power drills. I feel like power tools are used a lot more in raising children than most of the stuff on my silly baby registry. Because heaven forbid any childhood toy or plaything not come as a pile of pieces and stickers that parents must assemble as a way to prove their love. It's like an animal sacrifice, but with more blood and tears.

This means every holiday or birthday becomes a dark time for parents, as they are forced to prepare all their children's toys for prompt play. Usually you're able to assemble the bigger toys (fueled by booze and sleep deprivation) before their reveal, but it's the smaller toys that can catch you off-guard. Grandma gives little Bobby an amazing toy he wants to play with *right now*. He has never wanted anything more in this life.

You are left to assemble said toy while your bouncing ball of wonder and joy stares down at you like a very disappointed supervisor. He really had higher hopes for your success in this position. And the stakes are high: when he realizes you don't have the kind of battery this toy requires, he might walk right out the door and ask the neighbor to adopt him.

Even the toys that don't require assembly still require a Houdini-caliber ability to extricate items from zip ties. Fetal heart surgeons may be the only people whose hands can perform more intricate work under stressful circumstances.

Vivian went through a phase when she was enamored with train tables. There was a big one at the library we regularly visited and another at a friend's house. She would stand around those little tables and methodically move the trains around the tracks, have the trains talk to each other, and generally be entertained by an inanimate object for hours. So of course we needed to buy one.

A quick search online led to the troubling discovery that this train table clocked in at 120 pieces. But never fear: since I'm getting smarter when it comes to this parenting thing, I looked on Craigslist before purchasing a new one. (My greatest dream for my children is to always find them preassembled crap to play with. This way, Mommy can hold on to her sanity for a few more days.)

Luckily enough, Craigslist indeed offered an assembled train table. It looked to be in pretty good shape, so I eagerly messaged the seller. He said I could come get it that evening. I was ecstatic, thinking about all the time I wouldn't spend throwing train tracks at the wall in frustration while attempting to assemble all 120 pieces. Just as I was about to head out to pick up the table, the man contacted me with the heartbreaking news that his evil wife had sold the table out from under me.

I wanted to throw all 120 pieces at her.

Moms on the Front Lines

SOME ASSEMBLY REQUIRED

I asked my MOFL if they had any horror stories to share about the various toys they've been made to assemble in the name of childhood fun.

Chipper Jen was not so chipper about this topic. "Oh my goodness, Christmas Eve has always been a nightmare assembling Santa gifts. Kitchens, bikes, cars, you name it! I drank a lot of wine on these nights. Buy used!"

Sarah B. made an amateur mistake. "We got a fireman/police station dollhouse from Costco. It looked assembled online! We opened it on Christmas Eve about 10:00 PM and didn't finish for at least three hours!"

Michelle has an unfair advantage over the rest of us. "The race car bed was a fun one. Luckily my husband is an engineer, so he is an expert at putting together toys, furniture, bikes, etc." Her husband is the only person I've ever met who is actually qualified to be a parent.

Deanna said, "When Kate was two years old we got a toy kitchen with a million little decals. I was insistent that we follow the directions exactly so it would look like the box. After about two hours, we realized that she was never even going to see the box and just started putting the stickers wherever I thought they looked right."

I encourage you to follow in Deanna's footsteps and try to limit the amount of poops you give about making your child's toy look perfect. (Especially if you're smart and destroy the box so there's no comparison.) Your kids don't care where the stickers are. And most likely they'll end up making it their life's work to remove those stickers, because they believe the stickers would look better on the dog.

Also, the odds are your kids will get bored with this damn toy in less time than it takes you to build it. Actually, if you really want a toy that is guaranteed to entertain them, dump out all the pieces you're supposed to assemble and instead just hand the kid the box. *Bam*: entertained until they're twelve years old.

Journal Entry

ASSEMBLING HOLIDAY JOY

We have purchased an adorable play kitchen for the child. She is finally getting to the age when she can be entertained by her own brain and some marginally realistic toys. This is very exciting. I really like the kitchen we picked out, because it isn't bright pink and screaming "Only girls play with kitchens!" We've picked a stylish gray kitchen that is nicer than our real kitchen. It even has a backsplash.

We are quite proud of ourselves that we ordered this gift so far ahead of Christmas Day. We will assemble it well before the normal Christmas Eve Frantic Night of Assembly and No Sleep, and we will feel far superior to all the other parents who aren't as smart as we are. God, we are good at this parenting thing.

We will assemble the kitchen while Vivian is taking a nap, then hide it in the garage until the magical reveal on Christmas morning. We kick so much ass.

We open the kitchen box and empty out the contents. I double-check the picture on the front, because it appears that we have enough contents to build an entire house, not just the kitchen. The instruction guide is 453,533 pages long, full of pictures, and in thirty-five languages. This kitchen is apparently a huge seller in Dutch-speaking countries. Who knew?

We tackle the task of assembling all nine thousand parts. While I try to read Dutch, Becky just randomly starts grabbing pieces and drilling them together. It is times like these that I imagine how incredibly bad the two of us would be on *The Amazing Race*.

➤

We do not work well together at all. Becky likes to barrel forward and figure things out as she goes. I like to fully understand every aspect of a project before attempting any barreling. As individual strategies, the two ways of doing things work fine, but when you try to do both at once f-bombs become the primary form of communication.

We scrape and argue and slooowly assemble something resembling the outside of the box. Hours pass.

Vivian wakes up from her nap. We are only halfway through this journey. There is no feasible way for us to clean up all the remaining parts of the kitchen and move the assembled parts out of the living room before she comes downstairs. Vivian is less than two years old and doesn't yet know what Christmas is anyway, so we forge on. She watches us. More hours pass. She's already bored with this toy.

Our new plan is that we will finish the kitchen and still move it into the garage. After ten minutes Vivian will forget that it was ever here, and the Christmas morning reveal will still be fun for her. After we finally finish the kitchen, it is absolutely adorable and Vivian loves it. As always, the sweat and f-bombs were worth it. Now to hide it until Christmas.

We go to pick up the kitchen and move it. It weighs approximately 348 pounds. Apparently that backsplash is heavy.

I should have mentioned I am pregnant and not interested in exerting any more energy than the very least expected from humans. Even that sounds exhausting. Also, it says somewhere that I'm not supposed to be lifting heavy things while pregnant.

The kitchen is too damn heavy for Becky to move alone.

So we do the only logical thing. We push it over to the wall and say, "Merry Christmas, Vivi!"

She smiles and starts cooking her first meal. Happy holidays to all, and to all a good night. In mid-November.

19

YOU'LL BE EXPECTED TO DO THIS AGAIN

You are a glutton for punishment

SIBLINGS ARE SO FUN

"You have to have more than one kid! Siblings are so cute when they play together."

"Yeah, they look really, *really* adorable."

$\mathcal{A}$T SOME POINT in the first month or so of your baby's life someone will have the audacity to utter: "So, when do you think you'll have another?" Mostly the question will be laced with sarcasm, but there will always be a teeny little bit of truth in the inquiry. There is an underlying expectation that you will start all over with another baby someday, and maybe even again after that. Even if at the time you barely look like you'll be able to pull off your first round without the aid of many narcotics and a world-class plastic surgeon to repair the permanently dark circles under your eyes.

During the first few months of my first child's life I was such a mess of emotions, confusion, sleep deprivation, and generally poor hygiene that the thought of having another baby at any point before I'd be able to afford fourteen nannies (and a surrogate) seemed out of the question. When people posed the sibling question I'd look at them and ask, in all seriousness: "How in the hell does anyone do this more than once?!"

But just as you're starting to feel as if you might have a handle on your first kid (usually between 12 and 218 months), you will start feeling pressure to start this whole game over. The pressure will come in the form of innocent requests from family members: "Give me more grandbabies!!" Or maybe from friends who have multiple children: "Two is so much fun!" (They are lying.) In my case the pressure came mostly from myself. The plan was always to have two kids, and I knew that the older (and easier) the first one got, the less likely I was to start over. What on Earth inspired this desire for more than one? I blame television.

I watch TV dramas that include large families with everyone gathered around a table full of grandparents, children, and grandchildren. Sure, they seem to have a crisis (or four) every week, but the idea of having all my grown kids come home for the holidays or Sunday dinners gives me the warm fuzzies. I am an only child, and my extended family isn't very big. I always thought I'd like to have a bigger family of my own someday, because it seemed exciting. But then after I had my first baby I realized I really only want the bigger family of *grown* children who come visit on Sundays and holidays with my grandchildren in tow. I'm not overly interested in actually *raising* all of those kids, however, which presents a bit of a logistics issue.

Outside of TV land, whenever I see families with more than two kids I want to take a nap after watching them wrangle their brood. Their lives seem so confusingly impossible to my brain that I might as well be watching a polar bear cross the street on a unicorn. How the hell do people have three or four or, oh my goodness, five children? There just isn't enough caffeine (or a good enough plastic surgeon) in the world to make that calculation workable.

Yet, right around the time my little Vivian turned eighteen months old, I got pregnant with baby #2 ("Dos," as we called him while he was in utero). Vivian had become so much easier than she'd been during her first year or so. Regular sleep patterns were once again part of my life. I could see a little more ease on the horizon. So this seemed like a perfectly logical time to start my way over another ginormous hill. Logic is not my strong suit.

But babies are tricky little things, you see. They grow out of that first year of difficulties into real live little monkeys who are bounding around your house with more joy in their step than you ever thought was possible in a human (though you've witnessed such in bouncing poodles from time to time). They start to say words ("Mama" will melt your heart on contact), laugh hysterically, and develop a sense of humor that rivals that of many boring adults you've been made to share appetizers with. And you start to forget that it was ever really really hard—especially since sleep deprivation has long since destroyed any hope of your memory protecting you.

Then they start playing with their stuffed animals and dolls—a lot. And you think maybe it would be fun for them to have an actual other human to play with. And maybe it would be beneficial for them to have a sibling when they are an adult. You want that for them, even if you also want sleep for yourself. So you give in. And you start Googling "face-replacement plastic surgery."

Also, and this was the deciding factor for us, our life was already over as a result of having one child, so why not add another to the mix to give her a playmate? I really think the most traumatizing aspect of having our first baby was the way she absolutely destroyed the precious freedom we had enjoyed for a very, very long time (please see Chapter 11: You're Too Old for This). That took our legs out from underneath us in a way we weren't quite prepared for. But now that we were lying flat on our asses, the second kid wouldn't have the same chance to bring us down, because we were already beat!

So, as you can see, we made our choice with a ton of love and devotion and joy—and no logic whatsoever. Basically, we were already an exhausted mess, so why not add another? Yay, solid decision-making skills!

BABY #2 (AND 3 AND 4)

I got a lot of diverse answers when I approached my MOFL about their decision to add another baby to the mix. Some of them were standard answers, such as **Sarah B.'s**: "We didn't start thinking about it until Drew was almost two. My biggest reason for waiting was that I wasn't ready to share my time with Drew."

Chipper Jen also wanted her kids about two years apart, managing to plan them with birthdays in the same month, and then decided two was her golden number. "I got lucky with a boy and girl! I did want three but decided not to push my luck! Maddyn is like having ten, so I'm good!"

Then there was **Kaysee**, who is insane. "We started thinking about it after about four months. At six months we decided we would not prevent it and when Xavier was seven months old I was already pregnant again!"

The only thing I was thinking about when my baby was four months old was what I could possibly sell to afford those fourteen nannies I so desperately needed. The serious thought of another child would have been enough to send me over the edge I was already teetering on.

Monica, however, takes the cake with her story of seventy-five children (or four, but after two it really must seem like seventy-five). Monica had a nine-month-old baby when she found out she was pregnant with her second child. "I cried for a few days when I found out I was pregnant. I had a baby still. But that being said, I got over it within a week and it has been the best thing for those two. They're nineteen months apart to the day. Best friends. Polar opposites."

Ahhh, a happy ending, yes? So happy, in fact, she decided to do it again. "So we took a four-year break and did the exact same thing again." Yes, you heard that right. After four years they decided to replicate their near-twins by perfectly timing their next two kids to be about nineteen months apart.

I just . . . there are no words for this.

Monica does admit that her household isn't always easy. "It's crazy, but fun. I pretty much have zero expectations for myself each day. Then, if I get anything done, I feel great! It's a stage. I recommend the spacing that I did. If I could've had twins I would've but it wasn't in the cards. I think no matter what, the baby and toddler years are tough, so plow through them with two. You're already tired, so get two done at once. Then the four-year break was what I needed physically and emotionally, and it was nice for my relationship with my husband."

Personally, I need a four-year break after just reading Monica's adventure. How she actually made it her life is beyond my comprehension. Of course, she did grow up in a large family, so children running everywhere is just part of her norm. I, on the other hand, being an only child, used to break out in hives when there was too much commotion from one kid chasing the dogs around the house. So adding another child might not have been the best choice for my skin.

I reached out to another friend of mine, **Nancy**, whose daughter is three years old. Nancy and her husband have been debating whether to have another child, and are considering all the real-life implications of bringing home Baby #2. I wanted to include her story here because more and more parents are deciding to have only one child, for a variety of reasons.

Where should I begin? The main reasons we're still debating whether we should have one kid or two are money and opportunities. I am an only child; my parents gave me everything (not money and gifts, but opportunities). I went to the best private schools in Mexico (bilingual from kindergarten to senior year), I was able to live in the U.S. for one year as an exchange student, and I lived in Europe for a year and a half. My parents paid for my full education (four-year university included). I want to be able to provide Sofia with the same opportunities I had. I would like for her to travel the world, meet new people, and learn different languages.

My grandmother says that things always fall into place and that I shouldn't be afraid, that I will be able to provide my kids with what I envision . . . But what if I can't?! The way I see it is, worst-case scenario, these are the jobs we will have for the rest of our lives. Right now as we are, we can provide our daughter with good opportunities. If we had a second child, it is very likely we couldn't provide them both with the opportunities we want to.

Also, the fact that we have no parental leave is kind of a mood-killer. Taking unpaid time off to be with my first baby took such a toll on our financial situation that, three years later, we're still recovering. But even after all that, I see how awesome Sofia is with babies and her cousins, and I think maybe I am being selfish for not giving her a sibling.

I love how much thought Nancy and her husband are putting into whether or not to have another kid. The logic they're employing is something very rare in most family planning. Kids are *expensive*, and that expense is definitely something to take into very serious consideration before popping out more babies. As Nancy says, "Working just to have enough money for daycare is crazy."

In study after study married couples say that most of their arguments are about money. Bringing more kids into the mix is only going to force you to stretch your budget even further. I'm proud of Nancy for taking the time to confront this reality before thinking about expanding her family.

There are other issues besides money to consider when filling out your "Baby Dos" pro/con list. As an only child I always wanted to have two kids so that my children would have a sibling. But as soon as we had Dos, I started realizing how much my parents were able to give me because they had only one child. As an adult I don't think about the material things my parents gave me so much as how much of their time and attention I received. Both of my parents worked full-time and yet they never missed any important functions or sporting events. I was involved in roughly 786 extracurricular activities, and they both took a deep and involved role in my education. They are very good parents, but I do wonder if they would have been able to be as actively present in the lives of more than one kid.

This is not to say that I don't love my Baby Dos with all my heart and soul, and that I don't thank the heavens that I am lucky enough to be his mommy. But of *course* things would be easier if we had stopped at Baby Uno, especially considering the fact that we are a two-career household and also want to be very present for all aspects of our kids' lives. I'd like to be as involved as my parents were for me—but the logistics of being physically present for multiple kids and all their different activities don't add up as altogether possible.

But I will say that as the kids get older, I see little glimmers of what their relationship can turn into. Daniel absolutely adores his big sister. And occasionally his big sister tolerates him for longer than four minutes. It's special. Ultimately my decision to have a second child was never about how it would affect me. It was always about wanting to give Vivian a sibling. And the good news is that someday they may be the best of friends. The bad news is that day probably won't be until long after they've moved out of my house. Fantastic.

20

POTTY TRAINING
IS THE SH!TS
And it's everywhere

PROGRESSION OF POOP

"Nothing to see here. I'm not doing anything behind this couch."

"Look what I did! Let's talk about it! Nothing is more interesting."

$\mathcal{T}$HERE ARE A few things to remember before you head down Potty Training Lane.

1. No child has ever done anything of any importance simply because the parent is ready for him or her to do it.

2. Your child will not go to college wearing a diaper.

3. In the movie *127 Hours* James Franco actually drinks his pee to help him stay alive.

The last one may seem a bit odd to mention, but I include it because I constantly reminded myself of that movie throughout Vivian's potty-training attempts. No, we weren't experimenting with a bizarre method that involved drinking pee. But we were experimenting with trying to get a child to pee in a toilet instead of her pants. Often that experiment led to her experimenting with peeing on the floor, or the couch, or me as I carried her to the toilet.

In these instances, when I was left to emotionally and physically come to peace with someone else's urine as a constant presence in my life and on my body, I would close my eyes and picture *127 Hours*. Various thoughts would float in my head. "You can drink pee, actually ingest it into your body. It's that sanitary. It is totally fine that it is covering your floor, hands, and life right now. Or that you just realized your pants have had someone else's urine on them for at least three hours. This is all okay! Totally sanitary!" I'd like to thank James Franco for his contribution to my overall sanity during this trying time.

Potty training can start for some kids (not my kids) as early as eighteen months and as late as four years. Determining whether your child is ready to potty train can be a mix of reading their signs, implementing a plan, and a good amount of old-fashioned luck. Some kids are super excited about the potty; some kids want nothing to do with that weird contraption. Some kids give you signs of being interested, only to change their minds after you've put on that first pair of underwear.

If your kid is getting more independent and coordinated, has started expressing more interest in the bathroom habits of others, and seems to be going longer stretches with a dry diaper, it could be a good time to potty train. Or it could be an absolute disaster. Good luck with that.

Vivian was a little over two years old when her baby brother came along. Having two children in diapers was not the highlight of my parenting years thus far. We wanted to potty train Vivi, but we knew that the disruption of a new baby was going to make it hard to spring potty training on her as well. So we waited a few months before we decided it was time.

My friend Jen had potty trained her kids using a three-day method whereby you basically lock yourself in the house, take the child's diaper off, and cover all surfaces in towels. At the end of the three days the person who emerges covered in the least amount of shit wins a prize.

We set aside three days to attempt this method, bought a little kid toilet for the bathroom, and stocked the pantry with reward treats. We had been telling Vivian for a while that we were going to say bye bye to the diapers because she was a big girl and big girls went pee pee on the potty. She had no interest in whatever game we were trying to play.

We spent those three days struggling with accident after accident, frustration after frustration. I'm not sure why I honestly thought my child would magically start peeing and pooping on a toilet just because I deemed it time for her to do so (please see item 1 in the list above). It was a failure of a three-day attempt, to say the least. I was so defeated. And also, just as when you see ants and then are convinced you feel ants crawling all over you, I could not shake the feeling that I was covered in pee and poop. This might have something to do with the fact that I actually *was* covered in pee and poop.

After that initial failed attempt, we changed our strategy a bit. Instead of putting the potty in the bathroom down the hall, we put it in the living room where it was easily accessible (but still on tile, because new potty-users aren't great aimers). This meant she could meander over to the potty without fanfare and experiment with sitting without feeling like she was missing out on anything. And instead of freaking out every time there was an accident, we would say, "That's okay, sweetie, no big deal, accidents happen, you're doing a great job."

Taking the stress out of the ordeal helped our sensitive kid quite a bit. As did offering her a treat for every trip to the potty. It got to the point that she would pee on the potty, go to the pantry to get her reward, then go back to the potty, to try to get a little more out. But we played along, figuring that all peeing on the potty was good peeing on the potty.

We also made a *huge* deal every time she went to the bathroom. There were songs and dances, clapping and high-fives. ("Pee pee on the potty, pee pee on the potty, pee pee on the potty, wipe your hoo-ha in the front!") The girl enjoys a song-and-dance routine, so needless to say she loved the excitement around her potty success.

I'm not sure how long that toilet sat in our living room, but I do know it was long enough to officially become embarrassing. And I do know that it was quite a while before Vivian did anything besides pee on the toilet. That was fun. Even though we offered her bigger treats for poops, she still wasn't committing to the idea.

Then all of a sudden, just around Christmas, a poop on the potty! She just randomly walked over, sat down, and did her business. And just like that, I was down to only one kid in diapers. It was the Miracle on Eastwood Drive.

So many of my parental frustrations subside a bit once I let go of strict expectations of how things should go or what timeline they should follow (see item 1 above). Things will happen when my kids are ready for them to happen. All their little milestones will get marked off their lists when they want to mark them off, not when an Internet search tells me they're supposed to (see item 2 above).

I find it important to remind myself of these things often, because it's so easy to get frustrated by a particularly bad development phase or delay. And potty training is one of those phases that can literally go to shit. So grab some goggles, surgical gloves, a few gallons of bleach, and *127 Hours* and get ready for the ride.

Moms on the Front Lines

POTTY PAINS

I asked my MOFL to tell me about their potty-training highs and lows, when they started potty training with their kids, and any advice they have to share.

Sarah G. has the best advice I've heard. "I recommend against it. Potty training sucks."

Michelle kept an eye out for the signs that her son was ready. "He was interested, would tell me before he needed to go, would go longer between diaper changes, was excited about 'big boy underwear,' and would use the potty when prompted. Once he did all those things, we did the three-day method. He was just over two and a half years old."

Vivian was also a huge fan of her big-kid underwear. Of course they make them with all her favorite cartoon characters, which is very exciting. Although I was hoping that she would feel bad about pooping on Dora, no such luck.

Karen let her girl take her time. "She was three years old when she was successfully potty trained. I tried the three-day method as well and it just created stress for everyone. One day down the line it just clicked for her."

Each of **Kaysee's** three children was potty trained at a different age. "For me the thing that worked best was allowing each child to do it on their 'own' timing. This way they felt in control. Once they were ready we stopped Pull-Ups during the day so they wouldn't regress!"

We also got rid of all diapers once we were officially on the Potty Training Train. This meant more messes for us, but it was important that Vivian not think there was any going back. She really didn't like accidents, and she really, really liked her reward treat, so eventually it all came together.

Dana is worried about her future. "Boys and the bathroom are a foreign territory for me. All I have been told is that when it starts with boys, your bathrooms start to smell like pee."

Sarah G., mom of three boys, is not helping. "It's true! The other night I woke Jake and Theo up with disinfecting wipes to clean *around* their toilet!! Their actual toilet is immaculate. The floor, not so much."

Sommer had some questions for our MOFL. "Any advice about peeing at night while sleeping? My son is three years and three months, he's a pro at the potty during the day, but he wears a diaper to bed at night. Also, any advice on how to get him to poop on the potty? Right now he holds it all day and poops right after I put him to bed (in his diaper) at night. Trying so hard to break him of that."

Some of the MOFL recommended that Sommer cut her son off cold turkey from his nighttime diaper, as he is clearly able to control when he goes to the bathroom. However, **Sarah B.** had the same issue with her son and doesn't think Sommer should rush it. "Some kids just aren't ready to go without a Pull-Up at night. Our pediatrician said it's totally normal for boys to take up until five years old to be potty trained at night. Drew got rid of his pull-up diaper at about four years old. Prior to that we had tried just undies. We ditched the water before bed, we got him up in the middle of the night to go. But he would still have accidents. So we put Pull-Ups back on and then he eventually just started waking up dry. But there was a year difference between day and night potty training."

Michelle offered advice about dealing with a kid who refuses to poop on the toilet. "My son was scared to poop on the potty. So I watched for his pooping signs and caught him right before he had to go. I put him on the potty when he couldn't stop it. Once he realized it wasn't scary, he had no problem going on the potty. I also used a reward every time he went poop for a month or two."

You will be so excited when everything is finally happening on a toilet. But I warn you that successfully persuading your sweet children to poop on a potty by no means suggests your work is done. They finally understand that big kids poop in the bathroom, yes, but it can be a while before they grasp the concept that going to the bathroom is not a group activity. The more the merrier, really. Also, in their minds it doesn't need to be an especially quick activity either. "Sit down, get comfortable, let's catch up while I'm crapping right in front of you. I'm so glad you're teaching me about all the socially acceptable bathroom habits I will need later in life."

Of all the things I've accomplished in my four years as Vivian's mom, I think my proudest moment was when she got on the toilet one day and said, "I need privacy, Mommy." Yes! You do!! Thank the Lord you need privacy!

I promptly went to the pantry and got myself a treat for all my hard work.

21

YOU MIGHT WANT A DIVORCE

Seriously

QUALITY TIME

"The kids are finally asleep. You want to sit in absolute silence and watch TV shows with cursing?"

"That is the sexiest thing you have ever said to me."

$\mathcal{R}$ECENTLY ONE OF my friends posted an anniversary update to Facebook: "Four years of married bliss!" I chuckled and said out loud, to my computer, "Yeah, because you don't have kids. Of course you're blissful."

This may seem negative (unlike the rest of this book, which is super upbeat) but it's a very real thing. Adding children to a marriage is pretty much the end of the "bliss" period. The friend I mentioned above doesn't want to have kids. That means she has a pretty good idea what her relationship is going to be like over the years. I mean, obviously every relationship has ups and downs, struggles and issues. I don't think it's humanly possible for two people to spend their lives together without discord at some point. But adding kids to a marriage changes everything in a way that most people can't really prepare themselves for. All of a sudden you're literally in a different relationship. One that has other people in it too. Very high-maintenance people.

I definitely found that the first year of parenting strained my relationship. But the strain was mostly similar to the strain you may feel when trying to keep your head above water in the middle of an ocean of pounding waves. While sleep deprived. We were exhausted and trying to figure out how to navigate our new lives as parents. In those first months, our priority was just to not drown.

Most of the time we used each other as flotation devices. As an example, I might say to Becky: "Please, can you get up and deal with the screaming baby so I don't throw her out the window?" The most work we did on ourselves as a couple was not to go screaming into the night, leaving the other to raise the baby alone. So, you know, really healthy, solid relationship work being done there.

And then, just as Vivian was starting to get easier, Daniel made his appearance, and we were once again swallowed by the waves of having a new baby. It was obviously easier the second time around, simply because we knew the waves were coming and had developed survival techniques during our first go (a.k.a. "Please can you get up and deal with the screaming baby so I don't throw him out the window?"). But still, that first year with a baby is an ass-kicker no matter how much experience you've had getting your ass kicked.

Once we worked through the initial shock and awe of back-to-back babies, other strains started to present themselves. I found that, while we spent the infant years trying to figure out our kids, we are now spending the toddler years trying to figure out ourselves. If that makes any sense.

We survived two rounds of pounding waves, and we finally made our way to shore, but now we have to figure out how to build a life on this new island. We are the same two people who began this journey together, but we are in a completely different place. So now we have to start from scratch, really, to start becoming who it is we are going to be: as a family, as parents, as a couple, and as individuals for the long haul. (I hope this island has an unlimited caffeine source, and perhaps a babysitter on staff.)

No longer do we have to make quick survival-based decisions about how we will parent. Now it is time to make informed decisions about how we want to parent for the years to come. And no longer are all of our decisions solely about parenting: we've started actually considering what is best for us, both as individuals and as a couple. It's a revolutionary time, indeed.

One of our biggest hurdles during this time has been trying to figure out how to successfully co-parent with two very different parenting styles—differences that became very clear when our first child started toddling. Priors to that, our parenting styles were pretty much the same: we both wanted the child to be fed, warm, and happy. Then, when the toddler years arrived, our parenting styles started showing their true colors.

That's when I became the strict parent and Becky became the fun parent. (Please see Chapter 10: You May Not Be the Favorite.) For a while this caused a lot of stress all around: I suffered as the Bad Guy, Becky saw me as a buzzkill, Vivian picked sides. Happy times.

Child psychologist Gail Marie Poverman-Kave says that this issue comes up a lot in families. She believes that parents need to present a united front for the sake of the children. "When parents are not on the same page, or at least in the same chapter, dichotomous parenting styles can emerge, causing all kinds of chaos for parents and children alike."

MOFL Kaysee and her husband have dealt with different parenting styles too. "We've definitely had a few scuffles about it, and have learned we have to compromise between our different styles. It's about respect. If we don't respect one another, then the kids will pick up on it."

Child psychologist Katie Hurley says parents in this situation aren't bound to whatever parenting role they've taken on. "Just because one parent gets more fun time doesn't mean the other always has to fulfill the serious role, and the fun parent needs to know how and when to dial back the fun factor and be serious.

There is room in parenting for two fun parents who also know how to keep the family on an even keel."

After it became clear that our conflicting styles were doing nothing to help our child or our relationship, Becky and I were able to develop a bit of a compromise. She started stepping up to the plate and actually disciplining the kids, and I tried to loosen up a bit. Also, our rule is to always have each other's back if one of us is laying down the law with a kid. It's hard enough to convince a child you are in charge without having the other parent swoop in amid law-laying.

This is just one of the issues that can arise as kids get older and everyone has to officially start settling into Family Life. Couples may have issues regarding money (or lack thereof), work balance (or lack thereof), sex life (or lack thereof), and so on and so on (with no lack thereof).

Gail Marie Poverman-Kave recommends communication between parents to keep things in line. "Parents can benefit from meeting with one another on a weekly basis to go over ways they want to approach parenting issues, from the most mundane and pedestrian to the most challenging and complicated."

No matter how hard a couple tries, some partnerships don't survive this period, and I can see why that can happen. You come out of the haze of having babies and you realize that, not only has your situation changed dramatically from when you started out this relationship, but you've changed as well. Maybe you've each changed in ways that don't seem to go together anymore. Or maybe you spent so much energy focusing on the kids that you completely forgot to focus on your relationship, and now things have gotten to a point that the two of you are so far away from each other, there is no getting back.

This is also the time when you start realizing that this whole kid/family/work/being an adult thing is really really hard and is going to be really really hard for a long time. And that none of this is nearly as fun as *Growing Pains* would have had us believe. Sometimes couples don't survive because one or both partners begin to think there is something better out there, or at least something easier. That maybe there is some magic family situation that isn't affected by lack of sleep, excess stress, and far too few hours in the day.

I'll save you all a lot of trouble by telling it to you straight: that easy life you remember and still long for is gone. Long gone. (The good news is, your memory is so bad you'll probably forget soon anyway.) The stress and exhaustion and frustration you feel every day? That is not a unique feeling. There is no family out there who sits around at night and thinks, "Man, that was an easy day! I'm so incredibly good at this parenting thing, and my partner and I have nurtured our relationship so well, that Oprah is going to create an entire show around us for Super Soul Sunday!"

But I have good news! If you are finding all of this to be really hard, that probably means you are doing it right. Isn't that wonderful? Parenting, good parenting, is a lot of work. If it's not hard, then you are probably not very good at it. Relationships—good relationships—take a lot of work from both parties. Especially when both parties would rather do a face plant into bed at 9:00 PM than spend time nurturing your relationship.

If you have kids you need to remind yourself that you are so incredibly lucky. If you're married with kids? You're living the dream. Granted, it's a messy dream, and ironically a dream that involves little to no sleep. But still, it's the dream. Every night after I lay my kids down for bed I take a few seconds and remind myself how thankful I am to have them. (Pro tip: feeling thankful for children works best when said children are sleeping.) In fact, I take a little time and list all the things in my life I'm thankful for. Just to try to reboot my brain a little after an exhausting day.

One of my MOFL, Michaela, shared a story about her life as a parent: "My husband and I drove to Berkeley on Sunday. We took the boy and the dog to César Chávez Park near the marina— beautiful. There we were, both the boy and the dog being good, us strolling in the sunshine hand in hand, and my husband said, 'This is what having a dog and kid should feel like all the time, but never does.' I thought that summed it up perfectly!"

I think Michaela's story reflects the main reason everything can feel so overwhelming at times. We were all expecting it to be easier than this (damn you, *Growing Pains*!). And then we start thinking maybe we are the only ones who are so overwhelmed, maybe we are doing something wrong, maybe something like a divorce would fix things. But take comfort in knowing you aren't doing anything wrong—we are all miserable!! Yay, comradery!

Yes, life as a parent is hard. But that doesn't mean it can't be fun too. Between trying to balance work and kids and friends and family, I feel like I spend my days barely keeping all my balls in the air. Or I guess it would be more accurate to say I spend my days deciding which balls are going to be dropped. But as hard as it is and as tired as I am, I still try to find the fun in all this craziness. A little bit of laughter can go a long way on a particularly crappy day. Especially if that laughter is coming out of a kid's face.

And kids are almost always up for having fun. We regularly have random dance parties after dinner, just because. I'll play the kids a wonderfully nostalgic rap song from the nineties and they will shake their butts as only completely uninhibited kids can shake. Sometimes, even though it's a pain to keep Vivian up past her bedtime, I'll pack her up and take her to a movie in the park on a summer night, because it's a fun date with my girl. And since Daniel loves stickers, I'll let him spend a ridiculous amount of time meticulously sticking two hundred stickers on my face and neck, because it makes him happy (and because this activity calls for me lying down). Sometimes we'll set up the plastic bowling pins in the hallway and let the two of them knock them down however they see fit. Often at dinnertime we'll randomly break out in songs that we've written specifically about our family and pets over the years.

All of this is small stuff, but you'd be amazed how refreshing a seemingly small thing can be to a tired soul. And Becky and I make sure to look at each other and give a little nod during these tiny moments of happy family time. We acknowledge in the moment why we are doing all this in the first place. And for a second we are bonded over how stupid in love we are with these two babies and with this little family we dreamt into being.

So, yeah, marital bliss has changed a lot since parenthood began, but it's still there—you just have to look a little harder for it. And sometimes you have to work a little harder for it. But I promise that it, and you, are worth taking the time to find it.

Moms on the Front Lines

STAYING MARRIED

I asked my MOFL for any tips they had on staying connected to their partner for the long haul. Many said they try to make date nights a priority, although few admit to being able to pull them off regularly. A couple of moms, including me, have regular get-togethers with other families. This is a great time to connect with your spouse and other adults while the children entertain each other by destroying someone's playroom.

Amy, mom of two, makes me want to move to her neighborhood. "We have neighbors who have kids about the same age. We started a supper club where one household hosts and provides the entrée, the other families bring side dishes, and one household provides the kid hangout. A grandparent comes and watches all ten kids for $10 per family. It is great because we are next door to the kids if there are any emergencies but we have our adult time."

I'm on my way over to Amy's right now.

Sarah G., mom of four, has always made her relationship a priority. "We have always used sitters so we can go out on the weekends, and we lean on family to steal a few weekend overnights a year. I also think the Christian church culture really encourages and supports healthy marriages. We've been in weekly couples' Bible studies for years, attended marriage conferences, etc."

Michelle and her husband are still trying to find ways to fit connecting into their schedule. "This is something we are constantly working on. Since my husband works so many hours,

>

it's all we can do to get the kids fed, bathed, and in bed before my husband falls asleep! When the weather is nice we go on walks as a family. My older son rides his bike and my younger son rides in the stroller. During those walks we're able to catch up on each other's day. When we make walks a priority, we feel more connected."

In our house we find that getting a night away from the kids is hard, especially if we've been working a lot. Even though we want to get out together, a lot of times we would rather be home with the kids after a long day away from them.

Jill, mom of twins, came up with a way around the evening struggle. "For the first six years of the twins' lives, we took one day a week to have lunch, catch a movie, do a bit of shopping, etc. We thought it was really important for the kids to see us/ our relationship growing and it was crucial for us to thrive and survive in our relationship as well."

Deborah, mom of five, says that in the rare instances she and her husband are able to get away for a date night, they just end up talking about the kids the whole evening. She has found hanging out with friends is actually the best way for the two of them to really relax. "Having super fun friends to spend time with has been the best! It keeps us from talking about work and kids the whole time."

Michaela, mom of one, has tried to include her kid in all the activities that she and her husband loved before they became parents. "Sam has been all over California with us camping and hiking, to concerts, sporting events, bike rides to local restaurants, on cross-country flights, to CrossFit, and kept up late at friends' houses. Sometimes I hate that we don't often get kid-free time, but getting out and doing what we love, despite the hardship of a toddler in tow, keeps us somewhat happy and kind of on the same page."

In our house, in addition to date nights and fun times together with the kids, we have started allowing each other to take a night or afternoon away from the family on a regular basis. That couple of hours or even a night away seems to rejuvenate each of us much more than date nights do. That we come back home a little refreshed can go a long way in preserving sanity of all of us.

So yes, I'm essentially recommending you spend more time away from your partner in order to nurture your relationship. Why I don't have a daytime talk show is a mystery to everyone, I'm sure.

PRESCHOOL PARKING LOT

"I just dropped her off
at school! I've been waiting her
whole life for this. And by 'this' I mean
'a nap.' Do you think I'll get arrested
if I just sleep in the parking
lot every day?"

$\mathcal{W}$ HETHER YOUR KID has been in daycare or at home, you'll likely start thinking about preschool when said kid is around age two and a half years. (If your tiny tot has been home with you, you probably started thinking about preschool when he/she was about six months old, ahem.) The choice of when and where to put your kids in preschool is one of the first major decisions you will make in regard to their education. So don't mess it up or they'll likely drop out of school when they're in junior high. No pressure.

There is more than age to consider in deciding whether your kid is ready for preschool. Preschool, in all its different incarnations, is a place for your kid to start getting ready for the real school down the road. Play becomes a little more structured, with a little more focus on learning. Preschools have different degrees of academics, but one of the most important aspects of preschool is the social skills taught.

When considering preschool ask yourself a couple of questions. How many days a week do you want/need? Preschools can vary from two to five days a week. Does your kid have the basic skills required of a preschooler? Is he or she potty trained (this is a necessity, usually). Can he feed himself without incident? Can she wash her hands and put on her shoes? And keep them on? Can he follow directions and stay focused on projects?

Child psychologist Gail Marie Poverman-Kave believes there is no one right answer to the question of preschool, and that the key is to find the best fit for your kid. "Daycare and preschool can be positive places for children if they are mostly focused on play and exploration as opposed to formal learning. While young children require a structured environment, one that is too rigid or inflexible can cause stress for toddlers, resulting in behavior problems such as defiance or acting out. Finding the proper fit for your child is crucial."

In our case our primary motivation for putting Vivian in preschool was socialization. She had been home with a nanny and with us for three years, and I thought it was time for her to get out into the world. She was a reserved kid who was made more so by not venturing much outside of her small circle of friends and family. Also, since her baby brother had arrived, I didn't feel that enough attention was being paid to her rapidly expanding brain. Babies are pretty boring, and I thought having her in a more structured environment with kids her age and teachers who were focused on age-appropriate learning would really take advantage of her constant curiosity. Plus, I knew she would be so excited to get a little time away from her annoying brother.

Gail Marie Poverman-Kave says, "One advantage of preschool, especially for shy or reserved children, is that it provides them with the opportunity to learn how to interact with others in a safe, non-threatening environment. Social skills are extremely important, and the sooner we can help shy children address their fears, the better off they will be as they grow older."

Initially I was really worried about my girl, because she was *so* incredibly shy. I worried that putting her in preschool would be traumatizing to her sweet heart, but I also worried that not pushing her outside her comfort zone would be setting her up for even bigger trauma when she entered kindergarten.

For a while I was really bothered by her shyness, as if it were some sort of personality deficit. Why wasn't she as bouncy and playful as the other kids when we were out and about? Why was she the only kid clinging to her mama's neck at the bounce house birthday party? Were we doing something wrong? How could we fix this?

Then I remembered how shy I was when I was a kid. You could barely get me to speak outside the safe four walls of my house. But inside those walls was a totally different ballgame. I was outspoken and funny and full of life. Just like my Vivian. Over the years, as my confidence grew, I found my voice in public situations (and really haven't shut up since). So, instead of worrying so much about trying to push Vivian to be more sociable, I just started telling her it was perfectly fine for her to be shy. I didn't want her to have to deal with feelings of shame on top of her shyness.

So, if it meant giving Vivian the courage to attempt it herself, one of her moms was always willing to climb into those ridiculous play structures not made for anyone over thirty pounds. I also stood in the back of many ballet classes—while the other parents were outside—because it helped her to know I was there. I acknowledged her fears and told her I was scared of things too, that everyone is scared of things, and that there is nothing wrong with being scared. Slowly but surely she has become more brave. And I say "brave" not because she has become less shy or less scared; I just think she is slowly learning how to push on past her initial hesitation. I was in my teens before I could do that. It's been amazing to watch her discover how much fun awaits just past her initial fear.

Child psychologist Katie Hurley has this to say about shy kids: "Parents tend to worry that kids labeled as 'shy' might not be able to make friends as easily if they don't begin preschool early, but that just isn't true. Quiet, introspective kids thrive one-on-one and in small play groups. Sometimes a couple of weekly trips to the park are all they need to begin planting the seeds of socializing. We are conditioned as parents to think that highly social is better. The truth is that paying close attention to personality and temperament and letting our kids thrive in their own way are really best for young children."

We took this advice. When Vivian was around three and a half years old, we felt she was ready to start preschool a couple of days a week. I made sure to tell Vivian's teachers ad nauseam about how shy my girl was, as if she were the first child in the history of preschool to be a little on the reserved side. So she would feel comfortable going potty, and not have an embarrassing accident, I left her Dora potty seat at the school (the kind that goes on the actual toilet seat so she doesn't fall in). I also sent a long email describing my child's personality and how best to help her have a positive experience. Because, again, these preschool teachers had never been around children before they met mine.

Gail Marie Poverman-Kave encourages crazy behavior like mine. "Daycares and preschools are usually very willing to work with parents and mental health professionals in order to address issues like shyness and anxieties in children, making this a supportive, nurturing environment in which these children can learn to face their fears and learn how to deal more effectively with them."

I might have gone a bit overboard, but it warms my heart when I see her teachers with Vivian now. The way they take the extra time with her and lean in to hear her speak, because she is still so much quieter than the other kids. She feels safe with them, and there is nothing more I could ask for.

Moms on the Front Lines

PRESCHOOL

I asked my MOFL about their preschool experiences, what they looked for, and the ages their kids started attending.

Carrie, mom of two boys, kept both of her kids home until age three. After moving across the country, she's had to go through the preschool-picking twice. "I just did this again and let me say, schools in Washington State and Florida are very different. In lots of ways. Washington tends to be a bit more Montessori-ish, even in the big box chain preschools. Florida seems the land of big box schools, and they are more geared toward prep for kindergarten than semi-organized play. I had a hard time finding a school in Florida that I liked."

Karen, mom of one, was able to find the opposite of a big box school. "Mikayla had been in an at-home daycare from four months to two and a half years when I moved her to a preschool. I think I looked at nine to eleven preschools. For me personally, I wanted a play-based preschool that still gave some academic structure but did it through play and not 'schooling.' I wanted something that encouraged her creativity in all aspects: theater, art, make-believe, etc."

Jill did quite a bit of research before landing on the perfect fit. "We looked at the traditional preschool, smaller in-home preschools, and co-ops. Kevin and I *and* our kids *loved* the co-op. It was great learning alongside our kids. We looked for a place where the kids really grow while not being pressured to do schoolwork. We loved the concept of social/play focus."

Brooke, a teacher herself, wanted learning without too much structure. "It wasn't until I did a few site visits that I realized it would be hard to choose. There were some with thirty three-year-olds in a class, and in one visit we saw the kids sitting with the teacher drilling them on flash cards (some parents may like this academic aspect). Overall the site visits and parent recommendations are what mattered most in choosing."

Jodi had her daughter in daycare until she was almost four years old, then moved her over to a preschool. "Preschool was a little more structured than daycare. They started doing more than just art projects and singing. I visited several preschools and liked the Montessori philosophy. The routines worked well with Taylor's personality. It is more individually geared learning so each kid learns at their own pace. They also do practical life skills, and I like that aspect. The children grew leaps and bounds together in one preschool year."

One of my MOFL hasn't put any of her kids in preschool and doesn't plan to. **Leah**, mom of three, says, "We are planning to homeschool, the first few years for sure at least. And the kids are involved in at least three activities during the week at church where they are in a class setting with other kids, so socialization was not an issue. But I have three kids under the age of five so maybe my house *is* a preschool?!"

I too considered keeping Vivian home and concentrating on teaching both kids any and all things they would learn in preschool. Then I remembered I'm a really really bad teacher. After we made our decision to put her in preschool I discovered an added benefit to having Vivian out of the house. While his sister is out and about, Daniel finally has a little one-on-one time he so rarely gets as Baby #2. We run errands, go to the park or Mommy and Me classes, or maybe even have a breakfast date. It's so fun to hang out with him alone, although he doesn't quite hold up his end of the conversation as his sister does.

Don't be afraid to find the best fit for your kids, whether that's enrolling in preschool as soon as the schools allow, or holding them back until they are ready, or keeping them home until you feel it's right. If you go the preschool route, do your research and find teachers and a program that you feel comfortable with. And then, after all that, write a long-ass email telling them exactly who your children are and how to best deal with them. Trust me, teachers loooooove that.

Journal Entry

MY BIG GIRL

Vivian is over three years old. It may be time to let her out into the actual world. Do you think it's legal to keep her in the house until she is forty-seven years old? I'm going to look that up.

My partner and I both work from home, so we've had childcare since Vivian was about one month old. In those three-plus years, Vivian has been watched by a nanny or her grandma three to four days a week. We've been lucky enough to have close friends and family willing to babysit for most of Vivian's life, and it seems to have been a good fit for our shy girl. When we've been particularly busy with work, or left unable to work because the nanny calls in sick, we've debated whether we should put her in daycare. I was in daycare from about age six months, and I don't really have any feeling about it one way or another.

I've gone and looked at daycares a few times over the years. I did several site visits, found one I liked, had Vivian do a practice day, and even filled out the paperwork. But I could never quite pull the trigger and actually drop her off. I'm not sure why. Each time I started going through the motions of signing her up for daycare, she was still not talking. Somehow dropping her off with strangers before she was able to report back to me absolutely froze me. It's a small possibility I am a little overprotective.

But come on, she's my firstborn, and the sweetest girl on the planet, to boot. She's shy, sometimes debilitatingly so. I was shy when I was a kid, I remember how scary everything was for me back then.

So we kept her home. Because I was shy when I was a kid. Solid logic.

But now she is three. She's not school-aged, but she can talk. And she is still so very shy. I want to put bubble wrap around her and homeschool her until she is forty-seven. But I have to be strong. So I can teach her to be strong.

I think it's time for her to get out of the house, to be challenged more academically, and to start interacting with other kids in a group setting. She's pretty good with her close friends, on a one-on-one basis, but groups of kids overwhelm her. I can't say I blame her; groups of kids make me break out in hives too.

I've done some research on preschools in the area and found one that I thought would be perfect. We make the visit there. It's on about an acre of land and has goats, chickens, and a garden. Vivian loves animals, so I'm hoping they will distract her from the group of children who will be there as well. I like the main teacher. She is loud and boisterous, and seems to really enjoy the fact that she has twelve three-year-olds running around her at all times. She may be medicated.

Vivian is literally attached to my hip the entire time we are there, as if she has done the quick math on the number of adults present and realizes that this is not a Mommy and Me class. I promise her I won't be leaving her today; we are just visiting her new school so she can meet the teachers and the animals. Once she loosens up a little bit, she cautiously takes in the school. She doesn't hate it. But she doesn't let go of my hand the whole time we are there.

I find the place in May, and although the school year doesn't start until the fall, they do have a summer program that runs for a few weeks. I sign Vivian up and we start Operation School Prep in full force.

We start talking about school all the time. We watch episodes of her favorite cartoons that feature school themes. We buy a backpack that is bigger than she is, which she wears with pride. I talk the parents of one of Vivian's friends into enrolling their kid in the summer program, so she will have a familiar face in her new environment. We are ready.

I may cry.

I take her alone to her first day of school. We load Vivian and her giant backpack into the car and wave goodbye to Mama and Daniel. Vivian perks up a bit. "Daniel isn't coming?"

"No, sweetie, babies don't go to school, only big kids."

Vivian is officially on board for school now that she realizes her pest of a baby brother won't be there. Siblings are so sweet.

Vivian's new preschool has a strict drop-off policy. The teacher stands outside the school and welcomes the kids, so the parents don't even have to turn off their cars. It's super convenient. But it's not gonna work for us on our first day. Mommy is coming in. And she is probably going to cry.

Vivian sees her friend, and they both walk into school together. This will be great, they will hold hands, and he will protect her. The second we get in the class, her friend ditches her and starts playing with the seven thousand toys in the room. So, Vivian is on her own. I point her in the direction of some fun toys. She hesitates. I promise I won't leave without saying goodbye. She is scared, but goes to the toys.

The summer program has a mix of kids, ranging from ages three to five. Vivian is not only the youngest, but she is the only one in the summer program (besides her friend) who hasn't been in the school before. Since her friend is off socializing with other kids already, she's the odd one out. I'm an a-hole for not thinking about this.

Just as I'm about to do the crying, the sweetest five-year-old on the planet goes over to my girl and asks her if she wants to play with some toys over at the table. Vivian follows her without saying anything. She doesn't have to talk, because her new friend

➤

is quite the chatterbox. I watch them play. Vivian is having fun, although still quiet.

It's time for me to go.

I go over to my sweet girl and tell her I have to leave, and that I will be back a little later to pick her up. Her face gets scared and her eyes start to well up with tears. Until the sweetest five-year-old on the planet interjects: "Yeah, that's how school works! I was scared too, but it's okay." Somehow Vivian knows that because this girl is so happy to be here, it must be safe. She goes back to playing with her toys and she is okay. I give her a quick kiss, but she doesn't acknowledge me; she is at school now.

I love that sweet little five-year-old girl and the parents who taught her to have such a kind, kind heart.

I walk out of the classroom and make it out the door before I start crying.

EPILOGUE

MY SON DANIEL is a little over eighteen months old. While he has been an early adopter of the Wrath of the Toddler, as he nears the Terrible Twos he's making a noble effort to up his game. Recently he added a tantrum to his repertoire that is unlike anything I've ever witnessed outside of a sci-fi or horror movie. I look at him and honestly wonder how such a wailing, ear-shattering pitch can come out of one little boy. A little boy who was just snuggling his forehead into my neck five minutes earlier. Exorcism seems to be my only logical course of action.

Before I can fully accept the sound coming out of his face, I have to move into advanced acrobatics mode to try to keep the child from crashing to the floor as he violently lunges out of my arms. He doesn't seem to understand that the wailing will most definitely get worse if he manages to succeed in his extrication mission, at which point his head will have an immediate interaction with the tile floor.

Even when he's not in Wrath Mode he can still be an undertaking. While his sister sits calmly at the table during meals, Daniel still announces he is done by throwing his spoon across the room. He also still likes to take food into his mouth and chew it up before he makes the decision whether or not he is going to eat it. When he's decided and it's a no-go, he just spits it out—chewed blob tumbling from his mouth—and moves on to his next offering. He's all class.

But.

I love this phase.

I really do.

Because this is the Angry Monkey phase. And you know what comes after that?

Blob ➤ *Smiling Blob* ➤ *Monkey* ➤ *Angry Monkey* ➤ *Actual Human Child*

With every scream and flail, every flying spoon and spit-out food mass, I am getting closer to meeting my Actual Human Child. How exciting is that?

I often say, "I can't wait to meet Daniel." Because although he definitely has a personality, I know there is so much more of himself he is waiting to show us. (Although, if we're talking tantrum repertoire, I think I've seen just about enough, thank you very much.)

I'm not a baby person, really. I loved my babies, but I love my four-year-old even more. Vivian is now a little person, and I love getting to know her more every day. She has opinions and a sense of humor and a personality that are distinctly her own. Almost every day, I look at this little person barreling through life and think, "I pooped her out of my body, and now she is a real person!" (I have a way with words, I know.)

Meanwhile, as Daniel adds more and more words to his vocabulary, and more and more skills to his abilities, I slowly get to see him becoming a real person too. It's not the most seamless of transformations (think Incredible Hulk), but it's pretty cool to watch.

The toddler years are a confusing cluster-f of a time for us and our kids. The kids want so badly to be independent, yet they are so far from that goal. We want so badly to guide our kids to independence, but sometimes we miss the days when spit-up and diaper rash were our biggest hurdles.

The other day Daniel decided he wanted to climb a large rock in our backyard. Occasionally he gets very interested in this rock, which really means occasionally he falls off this rock. Over the past few months he's had a lot of spills off this rock, onto a very unforgiving ground. After each fall he screamed loudly and I scooped him up to comfort him. But he's not big on retaining lessons, so on this day he was going to battle the rock again.

I knew better than to take him off the rock, because unless I was planning on moving to a new house I wouldn't be able to deter his interest in this climb. So I stood behind him and offered my hand for help, as I've done countless times before. He promptly slapped it away, obviously.

He was focused and deliberate in his climb, taking time to balance himself and plot his foot placement. When he got to the top of his three-foot ascent he turned around to sit and enjoy his view. His swivel to put his butt down was wobbly at best. I quickly put my hand down, a few inches from his body, to catch him when he fell. But he didn't fall. He steadied himself and smiled widely, as if to say, "Look, Mom! No head injuries!"

Then he promptly slid down the rock and started climbing again, because that was amazing. Just then his sister came bounding in, jumped on top of the rock, spun around like a ballerina, and jumped off again. I could see the wheels turning in Daniel's head. I realized I'm going to be standing by this rock for a really long time.

But that's the gig, right? I would love to be able to stand near him forever, always offering a hand, always being there to catch him if he falls. It won't be long before he not only shoos my hand away but is far out of my reach. There will be so many times when scooping him up in my arms won't make everything okay. So today, I'm happy to stand by the rock, for as long as he'll let me.

Yeah, the toddler years are hard, and at times even infuriating. But we are building entire people here. No one said it was going to be easy. So we stand there, we watch them climb, fall, cry, repeat. We offer them our hand to help, we scoop them up and give them kisses when they allow it, we give them a supportive "Good fall, bud!" when we know all they need is a little encouragement to try again. We sacrifice our upholstery during potty training, our eardrums during wailing tantrums, and our sanity just trying to get out the blasted door in a timely fashion every morning.

We do all of this because that's the gig. And because we love our little angry monkeys more than anything on the planet. Even when they throw their bananas.

Because their giggles brighten our days, their hugs fix things we never knew were broken, and a simple "I wuv you, Mommy" can wrap its way around our hearts such that our brains forget all tantrum traumas that have come before.

Be gentle with your angry monkeys during the toddler years—and, more importantly, be gentle with yourself. Find the good in this time and cling to it with all your might. Hold them longer than you should if they fall asleep in your arms. Get down in the dirt with them and play mindlessly with pebbles for an hour. Color, bake, Play-Doh, and sing with abandon. Make a mess. Make noise. Dance.

And always, always, always remember: this is nothing compared to what's in store during their teenage years. Cheers!

See you out on the front lines, ladies. (I'll bring the wine.)

ACKNOWLEDGMENTS

To my agents Lilly Ghahremani and Stefanie von Borstel, for always fighting for me and for doing all the heavy lifting, so I can concentrate on making poop jokes. To Seal Press, for being my home from the very beginning, and for helping an unknown author grow over the years.

To Katie Hurley and Gail Marie Poverman-Kave, for their in-depth, thoughtful, and professional opinions. They really classed up the place with their knowledge.

To my Moms on the Front Lines (Amy, Brooke, Carrie, Colleen, Dana, Deanna, Deborah, Elissa, Heather, Chipper Jen, Jenine, Jill, Jodi, Karen, Kaysee, Leah, Michaela, Michelle, Monica, Nancy, Rachel, Salpy, Sarah B., Sarah G., Sommer, and Tara) for once again offering honest and unflinching opinions on whatever topics I threw their way. Whether or not I'm writing a book, they are my first stop for all things mom, and I'm so lucky to have all their brains at my disposal (even though, admittedly, all our brains have seen better days).

To Catherine Roe, for taking such good care of my babies three days a week. She fills those days with fun, learning, and adventures. They love her so much.

To my parents, Betty Lou and Dave Dais, who taught me by example how to be a good parent. My kids are so incredibly lucky that their amazing grandparents are such a big part of their lives.

To Becky Rook, for her love and support on this crazy ride. Even though it's hard, messy, and exhausting, I love our little family with all my heart.

To Vivian Lucia and Daniel Paul, for your giggles, your excitement, and your innocence. For those moments when you play peacefully together, the moments you run across the room to crash into my hug, and the moments you both randomly decide to sleep in on the same morning.

Thank you.

© Dawn Dais Wrangling Her Kids and Then Photoshopping Them Into One Suitable Photo Photography

*D*AWN DAIS IS a freelance writer and graphic designer. Her previous books include *The Sh!t No One Tells You: A Guide to Surviving Your Baby's First Year* and *The Nonrunner's Marathon Guide for Women*. She lives in Roseville, California, with her partner, Becky, their kids Vivian and Daniel, their two very needy dogs, and two rather moody cats. She is tired.

Stalk Dawn online at www.dawndais.com.

author photo © Dan Hood Photography

SELECTED TITLES FROM SEAL PRESS

While the Gods Were Sleeping: A Journey Through Love and Rebellion in Nepal, by Elizabeth Enslin. $16.00, 978-1-58005-544-4. An unexpected, intimate story of life in Nepal—and what happens when women confront society to defend their own human rights.

Wanderlust: A Love Affair with Five Continents, by Elisabeth Eaves. $16.95, 978-1-58005-311-2. A love letter from the author to the places she's visited—and to the spirit of travel itself—that documents her insatiable hunger for the rush of the unfamiliar and the experience of encountering new people and cultures.

Things No One Will Tell Fat Girls, by Jes Baker. $16.00, 978-1-58005-582-6. With smart and sassy eloquence, veteran blogger Jes Baker calls on women to be proud of their bodies, fight against fat-shaming, and embrace a body-positive worldview.

Fast Times in Palestine: A Love Affair with a Homeless Homeland, by Pamela J. Olson. $16.00, 978-1-58005-482-9. A powerful, deeply moving account of the time Pamela J. Olson spent in Palestine—both the daily events that are universal to us all (house parties, concerts, barbecues, and weddings) as well as the violence, trauma, and political tensions that are particular to the country.

The Other Side of Paradise: Life in the New Cuba, by Julia Cooke. $17.00, 978-1-58005-531-4. A young American journalist shares her experience of living in Havana and offers an evocative and revealing look at Cuba's youth culture.

Gorge: My Journey Up Kilimanjaro at 300 Pounds, by Kara Richardson Whitely. $17.00, 978-1-58005-559-8. In this inspiring and unforgettable memoir, Kara Richardson Whitely recounts her journey to the top of the world while struggling with food addiction and fat prejudice.

FIND SEAL PRESS ONLINE
www.sealpress.com
www.facebook.com/sealpress
Twitter: @SealPress